How Fat

was

Henry VIII?

HOW FAT
was
HENRY
VIII?

And Other Questions
on Royal History

RAYMOND LAMONT-BROWN

Cover: an original illustration by Gwen Burns

First published 2008
This edition first published 2016

The History Press Ltd
The Mill, Brimscombe Port
Stroud, Gloucestershire, GL5 2QG
www.thehistorypress.co.uk

British Library Cataloguing in Publication Data.
A catalogue record for this book is available from the British Library.

ISBN 978 0 7509 6626 9

Typesetting and origination by The History Press
Printed in Great Britain by TJ International Ltd, Padstow, Cornwall

Contents

Contents

Introduction

Whenever God of his infinite goodness shall call me out of this world, the tongue of malice may not paint my intentions in those colours she admires, nor the sycophant extoll me beyond what I deserve. I do not pretend to any superior abilities, but will give place to no one in meaning to preserve the freedom, happiness and glory of my dominions and all their inhabitants, and to fulfill the duty to my God and my neighbour in the extended sense.

King George III (r. 1760–1820) making a self-assessment.

The mystique of royalty, in the sense of its remoteness from the ordinary, has vanished in the twenty-first century. This is partly because of the burgeoning technological media available to pry into every corner of existence, as well as the lowering of deference and respect for the Royal Family. The trend of lowering deference is nothing new. Such publications as *Tomahawk* and *Punch* were sending up Queen Victoria and her family in the nineteenth century, following the spirit of *Atlas* which offered to the public royal epigrams of Queen Victoria's ancestors by those such as Walter Savage Landor (1775–1864) in 1855:

> George the First was always reckoned
> Vile, but viler George the Second;
> And what mortal ever heard
> Any good of George the Third?
> When from the earth the Fourth descended
> God be praised, the Georges ended!

In the twentieth century the Georges were back again. By and large George V and George VI received a better press. Although George V's court was described by the novelist H.G. Wells as 'alien and uninspiring', George retorted that, 'I may be uninspiring, but I'll be damned if I'm an alien'. George VI was also described as 'bumbling'.

Many an English and Scottish monarch have made blunders, played on by detractors. Edward II learned nothing from his affair with Piers Gaveston for instance; Elizabeth I made a terrible mistake in executing Mary, Queen of Scots, who in turn had brought death closer through her diplomatic blunders; James IV of Scotland took his army to destruction at the Battle of Flodden in 1513 by taking on his brother-in-law Henry VIII; by forcing the future Edward VII into a strict educational mould for which he was not suited, Queen Victoria and Prince Albert made their son a self-indulgent roué. The list is endless.

Even so monarchs have emerged from history as 'heroes'. King Alfred, who unified the country, was the only English monarch with the suffix 'Great'; Edward I also promoted the unity of Britain; in Scotland, Robert I, the Bruce, caused the nation to be accepted as an independent country; Edward III has been singled out as 'the greatest warrior of his age'; while Henry VIII put an end to medieval England and set in motion a social, economic and religious reformation, on which his daughter Elizabeth I honed a new backbone for England internationally. All these monarchs and more, individually and directly, made the nation what it was to become.

But human nature delights in things that go wrong. One guest at Edward I's coronation in 1272 was Alexander III of Scotland, who on hearing that there was an abundance of fine food, rode in with 100 Scottish knights. When the knights dismounted to pay honour to Edward I, people in the crowd stole their horses. Many royal weddings also had farcical aspects. When Frederick Louis, Prince of Wales, was married in 1736, his father George II, who loathed him, decided to humiliate him and his new bride Augusta, daughter of the Duke of Saxe-Coburg. While the rest of the family enjoyed the wedding dinner the couple were banished to the royal nursery.

All in all the story of the monarchs of Britain is the story of the nation itself. Their lives, fads, fallacies, victories, defeats, enemies, strengths and weaknesses are all threads from which British history is woven. This book sets out to give a taster of many of these aspects to underline how the public fascination with royalty never dims.

Royal Conundrums

How fat was Henry VIII?

> Fat Henry sat upon the throne
> And cast his eye on ham sir.
> No, no, Sir cook, I do propone
> I think I'll have the lamb sir.
>
> *Nineteenth-century nursery rhyme.*

The biographer of the sixteenth-century historian and philosopher, Edward, 1st Baron Herbert of Cherbury, pointed out to the world that Henry VIII 'laboured under the burden of extreme fat and [an] unwieldy body'. Luckily the king was dead at the time of the pronouncement, or the scribbler would have felt the edge of the axe that had decapitated two of Henry's wives.

King Henry VIII's reign, from 1509 to 1547, stood at the centre of a cultural revolution in England, in which food preparation was to play a prominent part at court as the country renewed itself in an age of Renaissance and Reformation. For six years a team of experimental archaeologists have studied the workings of the Tudor kitchens at Hampton Court, the palace on the River Thames which Henry acquired from his doomed Lord Chancellor Thomas Wolsey in 1528. Hampton Court's kitchens formed a complex of 55 rooms, worked by a staff of around 200, serving twice-daily meals for a court of 600 people. Records show that in one year Henry's courtiers consumed 1240 oxen, 8200 sheep, 2330 deer, 760 calves, 1870 pigs, 53 wild boar, a multitude of fish species from cod to whale, a plenitude of fowl, from swans to peacocks, washed down with 600,000 gallons of ale. Food played an important part in Henry's profile as a sumptuous Renaissance prince and in the impressing of foreign diplomats and visitors. Henry VIII as a gargantuan trencherman exhibited a personal assertion of national independence in Catholic Europe and a front for Tudor state power. It is likely, too, that Henry increased his 'comfort eating' on the death of Jane Seymour, his third wife and love of his life, on 24 October 1536, twelve days after the birth of her son.

Physically Henry VIII was 6ft 2in tall and his well-built frame became massively fat as he grew older. As a youth – he was 18 when he came to the throne – he was a pale-skinned, blue-eyed, auburn-haired charmer of 'fair countenance'; one Venetian visitor remarked 'His Majesty is the handsomest potentate I ever set eyes on' and a vigorous player of tennis, rider of horses and a skilled wrestler. And the Spanish ambassador noted that Henry's 'limbs were of gigantic size'. A study of his suits of armour in the Tower of London and elsewhere show that by 1512 the king had a 32in waist, which increased in the early 1520s to 35in, thence 54in in 1545. His portraits also show his swelling to fatness, wherein Cornelys Matsys's 1544 portrait of him shows Henry with cheeks sagging pendulously with fat, and his eyes and mouth mere slits within bulbous swellings.

From the 1540s Henry suffered from increasing periods of ill health. He endured ulcers for many years, eventually in both legs. Commentators have supposed that these were a result of syphilis, but no evidence for the diagnosis has ever been offered. Certainly the records of his chief apothecaries, Richard Babham, Cuthbert Blackeden and Thomas Alson, show no administrations of the then treatment – mercury. None of his wives or known mistresses had the disease and his children showed no evidence of congenital syphilis. In fact, the ulceration could have come about through varicose veins, or damage through jousting accidents or at the hunt. Henry had periods of remission, then agonising swelling and discharge; he also became depressed and the pain added to his scary, unpredictable temper. Henry's biographer, Edward Hall, also pointed out that by 1528 Henry suffered from bladder trouble and water retention. In all this exercise was made more difficult and Henry put on weight rapidly. By 1546 he could hardly walk; he was carried inside and out in a set of wooden, velvet and gold-decorated specially constructed chairs called 'trams', probably like the later sedan chairs. He had to be winched onto his horse and his armour was cut open to accommodate his swollen legs. Leg bandages oozing stinking pus from his ulcers caused courtiers to always remember their scented pomanders.

Henry died at Whitehall Palace at around 2 o'clock on the morning of Friday 28 January 1547 at the age of 55. The king's cadaver lay in its anthropoid lead coffin within a 6ft 10in elm chest in the Privy Chamber prior to its lowering into the vault in St George's Chapel at Windsor; it took sixteen Yeomen of the Guard 'of exceptional height and strength' to manoeuvre the coffin. It is recorded that during a funeral service at the Bridgettine monastery of Syon Abbey, Isleworth, Middlesex, en route for Windsor, Henry's coffin burst open spreading 'offensive matter', and filling the chapel with 'a most obnoxious odour'. Dogs were discovered soon after licking up the monarch's remains. In 1813 the vault was opened at Windsor and Henry's coffin was seen to have 'gaped open' to reveal his 'awesome skeleton'. It seems that the king's heart and viscera, removed during the process of embalming, remained in London, to be buried in the chapel of Whitehall Palace.

If a death certificate had been issued for the psychotic, paranoid bully that was Henry VIII, modern medical historians would suggest that entries could include amyloid disease, Cushing's syndrome (i.e. abnormality of the adrenal glands), chronic nephritis with uraemia and gravitational ulcer of the leg. It is estimated that Henry had a BMI of 35 and probably weighed between 25–30 stones. Thus today, Henry would be described as being morbidly obese; its cause a matter of learned opinion.

Did King Canute harness the waves?

Thou, too, art subject to my command, as the land on which I am seated is mine; and no one has ever resisted my commands with impunity. I command you, then, not to flow over my land, nor presume to wet the feet and robe of your lord.

Henry of Huntingdon, History of the English.

Canute, known to modern historians as Cnut, erstwhile Viking king of Denmark and of Norway, was crowned King of England at Old St Pauls on 6 January 1017. He was the first Dane to be crowned King of England, although his father Swegen 'Forkbeard' had conquered the land in 1013 and was elected king. Canute was married twice; first to Elfgifu of Northampton, daughter of Alfhelm, ealdorman (i.e. district governor) of Northampton, then to Emma of Normandy, widow of Athelred II 'The Unready', King of the English. Canute married Emma ostensibly to strengthen his right to the English throne; this he did while married to Elfgifu, who remained his 'handfast' wife (i.e. common-law wife) in accordance with Scandinavian law.

Documents about Canute's early reign are few and although the skalds of the Scandinavian world portrayed him as a great warrior, several chroniclers are prejudiced against him. He is portrayed as tyrannical, systematically murdering or banishing the prominent nobles of Saxon England. Nevertheless, he kept several Saxon nobles on his side who he elevated, such as Godwin, Earl of Wessex, to a powerful position. He also cultivated Wulfstan, Archbishop of York and Lyfing, Archbishop of Canterbury, and with the former he issued law codes based on those already promulgated by the Saxon kings.

Canute enters British folklore with the story of him sitting on his throne on the beach and commanding the tide to turn. The popular legend suggests that Canute wanted to show his people, enemies and continental neighbours that he had authority over the waves; the implications being that he controlled the northern waters of Europe. After all, he had commanded the Danish fleet in his father's time. This would certainly be the slant given by those who wished to make him out as an arrogant, harsh ruler who wanted to rule and repress. Yet there was another and more plausible side to the story.

By the 1020s, Canute had mellowed his former rule and had swung towards piety. His interest in church music caused him to compose a song for the Benedictine monks to sing as he and his knights rowed past their priory on the Isle of Ely:

> Merrily sung the monks in Ely,
> When Cnut the king rowed thereby;
> Rowed knights near the land,
> And hear we these monks sing.

He gave considerable donations to the Church – particularly Christchurch (Canterbury) – in the hope of buying salvation for his soul. Thus in trying to command the waves he was piously indicating that he did not have power over nature. More than this, too, he was reminding obsequious courtiers, who had suggested that even the waves would recede at his command, of his mortality.

According to Henry of Huntingdon (*c.* 1084–1155), in his *Historia Anglorum*, as the waves soaked Canute's feet he rose from his throne and addressed his assembled companions thus: 'Let all men know how empty and worthless is the power of kings, for there is none worthy of the name, but He whom heaven, earth and sea obey by eternal laws.' Thereafter, noted the biographer Goscelin (fl.1099), he discarded his gold crown, as a sign of humility, and placed it on the figure of Christ crucified at Winchester Minster.

Where these events were supposed to take place is a matter of dispute. Traditionally they are sited at Bosham on England's south coast. Yet a much earlier account by the Norman author of *Lestorie des Engles*, Geoffrey Gaimar (fl.1140) – who does not refer to Canute sitting on a throne – sets the events in the estuary of the Thames.

Canute died of a terminal illness at Shaftesbury, Dorset, on 12 November 1035. He was aged around 50 and his body was buried at the Old Minster, Winchester. His bones today are in one of the painted wooden chests at Winchester Cathedral on top of the choir screen in the presbytry, mingled with those of Saxon and Danish kings. As a monarch who conquered, established and ruled one of the most powerful of all Scandinavian empires, Canute showed himself to be one of the most important rulers of the day, whose potent sovereignty was universally recognised. So the story of the waves may have had an element of truth when chroniclers wished to portray the background to Canute's authority. Today the story is cited as an instance of futility and ignorant arrogance.

Why did Charles II hide in an oak tree?

A TALL DARK MAN ABOVE TWO YARDS HIGH
Rump Parliament poster appeal for the capture of Charles II
after the Battle of Worcester, 1651.

Boscobel House, Shropshire, lies where the old Forest of Brewood covered the area, 9 miles north-west of Wolverhampton. It was built around 1630 by John Giffard as a hunting lodge and its name derives from the Italian *bosco bello* (beautiful wood). The family of Giffard was Roman Catholic at a time when non-attendance of Church of England services fell foul of heavy fines and Roman priests were in danger of execution if caught. Indeed a member of the Giffard family had acted as a double-agent in the Babington Conspiracy (1586), which intended the murder of Elizabeth I and the installation in her place of the Scotto-French Mary, Queen of Scots. The plotters were duly punished and Mary, Queen of Scots was executed in 1587. At the time of Charles II's flight from the Battle of Worcester, Boscobel House was rented to a Roman Catholic family of farmers, the Penderels, so Boscobel's owner, Charles Giffard – one of the king's fleeing party – suggested they make for the isolated Giffard 'safe house' of Whiteladies further on. By Kidderminster and Stourbridge the fleeing royal party arrived at Whiteladies (now ruined) at dawn, 4 September 1651.

The king was disguised as one 'Will Jones', a woodman, in a 'green jerkin, grey cloth breeches, leather doublet and greasy soft hat'; his 'royal clothes' were disposed of. As Cromwellian troops were in the vicinity looking for fugitives from the battle, Charles hid in woodland, his aristocratic retainers having now dispersed. The king would be safest travelling with few retainers, one of which was Richard Penderel. By 9 September Cromwell had placed a price of £1,000 on the king's capture. No one ever claimed the prize. As they made their way from Whiteladies in the direction of the Severn, Charles and Penderel dodged troopers and, frugally fed by trusted Penderel tenants, they decided that there were too many hazards in their path and they must make for Boscobel House and the comparative safety of the Penderel household.

What were the events that brought Charles II to Boscobel House? Charles Stuart was the eldest surviving son of Charles I and his queen Henrietta Maria, daughter of Henry IV of France. He was born at St James's Palace, London, on 29 May 1630. After a safe childhood in the magnificence of his father's palaces, Charles was 12 when the Civil War broke out. Quickly he became proficient in military activities and at the age of 14 he was in command of Royalist troops in the West Country. The tide of war swung against the Royalists and, following the loss of Hereford and Chester in 1645, Charles heeded his father's advice and fled to France via the Scilly and Channel Islands to reach his exiled mother in Paris. By 1648 he was in Holland, where his sister Mary, the Princess Royal, had married William, Prince of Orange. Here Charles had a dalliance with Lucy Walter (d.1658), who bore him a son James in 1649; the child went on to be Duke of Monmouth. While in the Hague, Charles heard of his father's execution at Whitehall Palace on 30 January 1649.

On 16 February 1649, the month before the new (republican) parliament abolished the monarchy, Charles was proclaimed king in Jersey, and a short while later the Scottish parliament proclaimed him monarch (if he was prepared to recognise the Scottish Covenant of 1638). Ever a man to bend with the wind, Charles agreed an ambiguous treaty with the Scots and, despite Cromwellian occupation of Scotland, he was crowned King of Scotland at Scone Abbey on 1 January 1651.

While Oliver Cromwell went on to show the Scots that he meant business, in July 1651 Charles led an army into England. On 3 September they were at Worcester; nearly 17,000 Royalists under Charles, with James, the 1st Duke of Hamilton and David Leslie, Baron Newark faced 28,000 Roundheads led by Cromwell, Charles Fleetwood, Col Thomas Harrison and Col John Lambert. Fierce fighting took place at Powick Bridge, south of Worcester. Battle raged for five hours, but Charles was driven back into Worcester city. He tried to rally his straggling, defeated troops. At length Charles was persuaded to escape by way of St Martin's Gate.

The Royalist cause was destroyed, but it remained to save the person of the king.

Charles II own version of the melodramatic escape from the Battle of Worcester was recounted to diarist Samuel Pepys twice; the first time was aboard the RY *Royal Charles* on 23 May 1660 en route to his triumphal restoration, then again at Newmarket races in October 1680. Although Sir Walter Scott enthralled his readers in a fictional version of the escape in his novel *Woodstock* (1820), the main facts of the events are these: On 3 September 1651 Charles vanished into the darkness north of Worcester with a small group of Royalists including George Villiers, 2nd Duke of Buckingham, James Stanley, 7th Earl of Derby and John Maitland, 2nd Earl (later Duke) of Lauderdale. They were heading for the sanctuary of Brewood Forest and then – recommended by Lauderdale and Derby – the 'loyal house' of Boscobel. So this is what brought Charles to the Boscobel policies.

Safe for a while Charles caught up with news of the aftermath of the battle and heard that Royalist Major William Carlis was hiding in the nearby wood. Carlis now joined Charles and the pair perched themselves in a thick foliated pollard oak from where they could observe the environs of the house. Later Charles recounted to Samuel Pepys: 'While we were in the tree we [saw] soldiers going up and down … searching for persons escaped.' The king was able to sleep for a while in the tree; although a cushion had been provided by the Penderels, the king's 6ft 2in frame was uncomfortably contorted. That evening (6 September), the king and Major Carlis descended from the oak and took refuge in Boscobel House. That night Charles rested in a priest's hiding place at the top of the building but the next day Cromwell's troopers were deemed far enough away for the king to walk in the garden.

This was just the beginning of Charles's tortuous escape plans: from lawyer Thomas Whitgreave's house, Mosely Old Hall, where troopers searched the house while the king hid in a secret room, to Col John Lane's home at Bently Hall near Walsall and then on to the Cromwellian-held Bristol. Dogged by bad luck no passage was available for Charles at Bristol and it was not until 15 October at 4 o'clock in the morning that Charles embarked at Shoreham for the Continent. Subsequent biographical details of Charles II are well known. He was restored to the throne in 1660 and crowned at Westminister Abbey on 23 April 1661. Charles ruled until his death at Whitehall Palace, 6 February 1685, aged 54.

Today a descendant of the original tree marks the spot of the dramatic affairs. A spin-off for these events was once celebrated as Oak Apple Day. Until the middle of the nineteenth century it was celebrated as a public holiday on 29 May, Charles II's birthday and the day of his restoration in 1660. Some fervent Royalists even wore oak leaves in hats and lapels, while others decorated house doorways with oak boughs. Charles also contemplated founding a new order to be called Knight of the Royal Oak, but plans were never set in motion. The tree, too, was an inspiration for the 'Royal Oak' inn signs.

What was the real relationship between Queen Victoria and her Highland servant John Brown?

He has been taken and I feel again very desolate, and forlorn … for what, my dear faithfull Brown … for he was in my service for 34 years and for 18 never left me for a single day … did for me, no one else can. The comfort of my daily life gone … the void is terrible … the loss is irreparable! The most affectionate children, no lady or gentleman can do what he did.

Queen Victoria to Alfred, Lord Tennyson,
Osborne, 14 August 1883.

20

One morning in September 1866 the British Minister Plenipotentiary, the Hon. E.A.J. Harris, based at Berne, Switzerland, opened his copy of the *Gazette de Lausanne* and was horrified to read the following:

> On dit [They say] ... that with Brown and by him she consoles herself for Prince Albert, and they go even further. They add that she is in an interesting condition, and that if she was not present for the Volunteers Review, and at the inauguration of the monument to Prince Albert, it was only in order to hide her pregnancy. I hasten to add that the Queen has been morganatically married to her attendant for a long time, which diminishes the gravity of the thing.

Queen Victoria pregnant by her Highland servant! Harris nearly succumbed to apoplexy. Without consulting the Foreign Secretary, Lord Edward Henry Stanley (later 15th Lord Derby), Harris made an official complaint to the Swiss Federal Council concerning the paper's allegations. The Swiss authorities did nothing. The Foreign Office was somewhat embarrassed at Harris's intervention and officially withdrew the complaint through the Swiss ambassador to the Court of St James. Nevertheless, Harris had given the scurrilous nonsense the oxygen of publicity it would not otherwise have achieved. Back in Britain, not even the socialist radical weekly *Reynolds's Newspaper* – certainly no supporter of Queen Victoria and the Royal Family – followed up the story. Where the allegations had come from is unclear. Some say they originated in Paris to be imported to Britain in French pornography, yet from such gossip branched a whole tree of slander and innuendo; its echoes still reverberating today.

Who was this Scotsman who earned the hatred of so many, including Queen Victoria's eldest son the Prince of Wales? Why did Brown play such a prominent role at Queen Victoria's court?

John Brown was born at Crathienaird, Crathie parish, Aberdeenshire, on 8 December 1826, second of the eleven children of tenant farmer John Brown and his wife Margaret Leys. He was educated at the local Gaelic-speaking school at Crathie and at home, and from 1839 worked as a farm labourer at local farms and as an ostler's assistant at Pannanich Wells. He became a stable boy at Sir Robert Gordon's estate at Balmoral and was on the staff when Queen Victoria, Prince Albert and the Royal Family visited Balmoral for the first time on 8 September 1848.

John Brown is first mentioned in Queen Victoria's journal on 11 September 1849 during the Royal Family's visit to Dhu Loch, the year he was promoted to gillie at Balmoral. By 1851 Brown had taken on the permanent role of leader of Queen Victoria's pony on Prince Albert's instigation. In 1852 the Royal Family bought Balmoral and a new castle was designed by Prince Albert, to be completed in 1855. In 1858 John Brown became personal gillie to Prince Albert. Until the prince's death on 14 December 1861, John Brown was a prominent attendant when the Royal Family were at Balmoral, particularly on the 'Great Expeditions' Queen Victoria and her entourage made to various locations in Scotland.

The mental decline into which Queen Victoria slipped for several years on the death of Prince Albert is well chronicled and in 1864 the queen's second daughter and third child Princess Alice, the Keeper of the Privy Purse Sir Charles Phipps and Royal Physician Dr William Jenner, met to discuss Queen Victoria's sustained depression and reluctance to appear in public. From this it was suggested that John Brown be brought from Balmoral to help remind the queen of 'happier times' on vacation in Scotland and to encourage the queen to go horse riding again. Thus, in December 1864 John Brown arrived at Osborne House as groom.

In this way began John Brown's elevated career at court. Slowly his brusque, no-nonsense manner increasingly appealed to the queen and a pattern of daily horse rides began. When the queen became too rheumatic to sit on a horse Brown took her out in a pony cart. She loved the way he fussed and cosseted her, as E.E.P. Tisdale remarked:

He came to take her for daily drives, morning and afternoon. He pushed aside bowing lackeys in gaudy finery. He was brusque with the ladies who fluttered like frightened chickens in his way. The carriage was his preserve. It was his task to see that the Queen was settled amongst her cushions, his horny fingers which must ensure that her jacket was buttoned against the wind, his hands which must spread the shawl about her shoulders. Others had tended her as their Queen and mistress. John Brown protected her as she was, a poor, broken-hearted bairn who wanted looking after and taking out of herself.

It was not in John Brown's nature to be subservient and his tactless, mischief-making and blunt overbearing manner soon got on the wrong side of many of the Royal Household, from the Prince of Wales's courtiers to the secretariat under Sir Charles Grey. Brown had his own idiosyncratic way of conveying the queen's instructions to her courtiers, often twisting her words from diplomacy to rudeness. Many were appalled too at the seemingly familiar way in which he treated the queen and was downright impertinent to the queen's family. Whenever they or her staff complained she would find some excuse to exonerate Brown.

By 1865 Queen Victoria decided to keep John Brown 'permanently' on her immediate staff and he was given the title 'The Queen's Highland Servant' at a salary that rose from £150 per annum to £400 by 1872. He was also awarded the 'Faithful Servant Medal' and the 'Devoted Servant Medal'. Over the years gossip, both written and spoken about Queen Victoria's relationship with John Brown, increased and it focused on four main topics: The queen had married John Brown; she had given birth to John Brown's child; she had gone mad and John Brown was her keeper; John Brown was Queen Victoria's spiritualistic medium.

The nonsensical assertion that John Brown was married 'morganatically' to Queen Victoria was first given the light of day by the socialist republican nationalist Alexander Robertson. He produced the pamphlet *John Brown: A Correspondence with the Lord Chancellor, Regarding a Charge of Fraud and Embezzlement Preferred Against His Grace the Duke of Athole K.T. of 1873*.

Robertson had a running dispute with the 6th Duke of Atholl regarding the payment of a toll to cross the seven-arched bridge across the River Tay at Dunkeld, Perthshire. The bridge had been built by the 5th Duke and folks complained that they had to pay the halfpenny return toll even when they went to church. Queen Victoria was a firm friend of George Murray, 6th Duke of Atholl and his Duchess Anne. Robertson assumed that the queen was a supporter of their 'banditry' with regard to the toll and was therefore ripe for exposure.

Addressed to the Lord Chancellor, the 1st Lord Selborne, the pamphlet detailed several accusations against the queen and John Brown. Identifying one Charles Christie, 'House Steward to the Dowager Duchess of Athole at Dunkeld House', as the source of his information, Robertson stated that John Brown obtained regular 'admittance' to Queen Victoria's bedroom when 'the house was quiet'. Robertson also stated that he was told that the queen had married John Brown at Lausanne, Switzerland, in 1868 with Duchess Anne as witness. On publication the duchess was quizzed about the allegation and poured scorn on Robertson's assertion. Even more fanciful, Robertson stated that Queen Victoria had given birth to John Brown's child. This time he said that his source was one John McGregor, Chief Wood Manager on the Atholl estates, who had told him that Brown and the queen had a love nest near Loch Ordie and there conception had taken place. The child, said Robertson, was born in Switzerland with Duchess Anne as midwife and the infant was given away to be brought up by a 'Calvinist pastor' in the Canton of Vaud.

Robertson's assertions were officially noted. He was never prosecuted for his libel, although the Lord Chancellor and Foreign Secretary, George Leveson-Gower, 2nd Earl of Granville discussed the implications of the pamphlet.

Not only her courtiers but the queen herself believed that she had inherited from her Hanoverian ancestors a proclivity to madness. The mental instability of her grandfather George III in his later life was readily quoted. The queen did suffer from what the 4th Earl of Clarendon called her 'morbid melancholy', and would sometimes display a certain agitation and hysteria when beset with problems. Consequently government ministers and members of her household would be easily blackmailed into doing what she wanted to avoid upset. John Brown understood this and his determined interference in her life was a help to tackle her moods. Thus to some this was interpreted that the queen was mad and that Brown was her 'keeper'.

With Brown being a Highlander it was presumed that he had the phenomenon known as *taibhseadaireachd* the 'Second Sight' with all its psychic attributes. As Queen Victoria was obsessed with the morbid memory of Prince Albert it was easy for gossips to conclude that the 'psychic' John Brown was her spiritualistic medium. All of these elements of gossip had deep roots and there were many willing to exploit them.

The gossip about Queen Victoria and her Highland servant did not just circulate among the nation's lower classes. Republicanism was given a boost by Queen Victoria's period of seclusion following the death of Prince Albert in 1861, and her consequent neglect of royal duty. Again there was an anti-royal prejudice that lurked in the bowels of the Liberal Party given credence by the likes of the radical MP Sir Charles Wentworth Dilke and pamphleteer

Goldwin Smith. At court factions muttered against the queen and those around Albert Edward, Prince of Wales resented the supposed influence John Brown had over Queen Victoria. Furthermore, John Brown's presence at court stirred up the anti-Scottish feelings in the Royal Household that had been present since the eighteenth century. Both Queen Victoria and her prime minister, the 14th Earl of Derby, believed that certain courtiers had leaked anti-Brown and anti-Victoria comments to such journals as *Punch* and *Tomahawk*, and Derby identified such gossips to include George Villiers, 4th Earl of Clarendon (Foreign Secretary 1865–66) and court painter Sir Edwin Landseer. All the leftist clubs and the likes of the (Irish) Fenian Brotherhood feasted on and promoted anti-royalist feelings.

Although much of the gossip about John Brown and Queen Victoria was seen as ridiculous, steps were taken to suppress information. For instance, when Queen Victoria died her daughter Princess Beatrice removed pages from the queen's journal 'that might cause pain' (ostensibly regarding John Brown); again on the queen's death any papers and letters regarding John Brown and the queen were destroyed on the orders of the new king Edward VII. Queen Victoria often peppered her letters with such words as 'darling one' and 'love', all used in a naive way; but these could easily be misinterpreted by anyone wishing to make trouble.

It is clear, despite public gossip and 'those horrid publications whose object is to promulgate scandal and calumny [about herself and John Brown] which they invent themselves', wrote Queen Victoria to Lord Tennyson in 1883, the year of Brown's death, that there was nothing immoral in Queen Victoria's relationship with John Brown. Queen Victoria would never have contemplated sex with a servant. Furthermore, she was never alone to carry out an affair, having court ladies always within shouting distance. The significance of Queen Victoria's attraction to John Brown was that he made a career out of her. He never married, had few holidays and devoted his life to the queen, and he was a walking encyclopaedia of her likes, dislikes, moods and needs. As a downright selfish person this greatly appealed to the queen. Brown was a true and faithful friend to Victoria, and despite his idiosyncratic attitude to his work and his drunkenness (to which she turned a blind eye), he was totally loyal to her. She liked him because she needed to be fussed, cosseted and spoiled. He told her the truth, spoke boldly to her and importantly too – unlike her family and senior courtiers – he was not afraid of her. Above all, when Prince Albert died Queen Victoria needed a male friend – she never really made close friendships with women – and someone to lean on. John Brown supplied all that.

Was Elizabeth I a 'virgin' queen?

I would rather be a beggar and single than a queen and married.

Queen Elizabeth I to the ambassador, the Duke of Wurtemburg.

Elizabeth Tudor scarcely knew her mother Anne Boleyn, who was executed when Elizabeth was 32 months old. Born at Greenwich Palace, 7 September 1533, the second surviving child of Henry VIII, Elizabeth was dispatched to Hatfield Palace, Hertfordshire, when but an infant. Her young life was a series of bitter rejections and manipulations. Her elder half-sister, who ruled as Mary I of England, disowned her, and although declared illegitimate when the marriage of Henry VIII and second wife Anne Boleyn was declared void, she was later dubbed legitimate and 'heiress of a kingdom' when her father used her as a barter piece towards a political alliance through marriage. Her aversion to being a pawn may have led her to view marriage with distaste.

Intelligent, precocious and very well educated for a woman of her era, Elizabeth lived through various vicissitudes in the reigns of her half-siblings Edward VI and Mary I, to be confined in the Tower of London, then Woodstock, near Oxford, when Mary took the notion that Elizabeth was plotting against her. Yet on Mary's death at St James's Palace, 17 November 1558, Elizabeth became monarch to general rejoicing in the land.

Elizabeth's reign to her death at Richmond Palace at 3 p.m. on 24 March 1603, aged 69, has become known as 'England's Golden Age'. Yet her reasons not to marry remain a matter of conjecture and her purported lifelong virginity survives as a mystery. For Elizabeth, it seems, the marriage issue developed as a clear choice; who should she *possibly* marry as opposed to *actually* marry. As an astute ruler, Elizabeth knew that a political marriage was necessary for two reasons; to produce a legitimate heir, and to strengthen England's role in Europe. As the most eligible woman in Europe, suitors came and went, from her former brother-in-law, Philip II of Spain to Charles, Archduke of Austria and even the bisexual transvestite Henri, duc d'Anjou, whose brother Charles IX, King of France had also been a possibility. The more she aged and the more she refused to identify an heir the more her government became nervous. They feared that if she died without declaring a successor, as a great-granddaughter of Henry VII, Mary, Queen of Scots would claim the rights of succession and plunge England into another bout of Roman Catholic oppression. In 1559 in particular parliament pressed Elizabeth to marry. The antiquary and historian William Camden – who was commissioned by James I/VI to write his cousin Elizabeth's biography – recorded her reply: 'I have already joyned myself in marriage to a Husband, namely, the Kingdom Of England.'

Delighting in flaunting her 'virginity', Elizabeth encouraged all to refer to her as the 'Virgin Queen', to the extent that Walter Raleigh named territory in North America in 1584 as Virginia in her honour. In all this Elizabeth flouted the opinions of the day. Shakespeare spoke for his generation when he wrote: '[Virgins compare to] one of our French wither'd pears – it looks ill, it eats dryly.' Since the Reformation virginity had lost its repute. The Protestant divine Thomas Becon, erstwhile chaplain to Protector Somerset, preached that virginity was inferior to marriage, noting that the old traditions of celebacy and virginity were 'Romish'. Publicly, at least, Elizabeth followed the ideas of Bishop John Jewel of Salisbury that chastity was a 'gift', and that her virginal state set her apart as a kind of 'elect'. Nevertheless people asked: How could a daughter of lusty Henry Tudor be a virgin?

Victorian historians, novelists and film producers in particular have identified who they considered the most probable contender for the queen's bed, namely, Robert Dudley, Earl of Leicester (1532–88). Others too, like Robert Devereux, 2nd Earl of Essex (1566–1601), have provoked scandalous speculation, but Dudley engendered the most. His roller-coaster career as MP, supporter of Lady Jane Grey, master of the ordnance and privy councillor, brought him to Elizabeth's court and his role of 'favourite'. When Dudley's wife, Amy Robsart, died in 1650, following a purported fall down some stairs, court gossips promoted the suggestion that she had been murdered to make Dudley free to marry the queen. Gossips claimed also that Elizabeth had borne Dudley a child. Was there any truth in this? To recount such stories was treason, so courtiers caught retailing them ran the risk of tongues and ears removed or the ultimate penalty of death. Elizabeth was an incorrigible flirt; during one ceremony in which she invested Dudley with his collar as earl, the foreign envoys were shocked to see her playfully tickle his neck.

Dudley's name was entwined with Elizabeth's once more in a curious tale set out by those wishing to prove that Elizabeth was not the virgin she purported to be. During June 1587, when King Philip of Spain was having an *Armada Grande* prepared for the invasion of England, a vessel bound for France was intercepted off the fortified Basque fishing port of San Sebastian. Among those on board was an Englishmen in his mid-twenties who told his interceptors that he had been visiting the Shrine of Our Lady of Montserrat in the rugged mountains near Barcelona. He was now making his way spiritually refreshed to France. Suspected of being a spy he was shipped to Madrid and imprisoned. Strangely for a person in his position his request to see Sir Francis Englefield of Englefield House, Berkshire, was granted. Sir Francis was a Roman Catholic exile from Elizabethan England at Valladolid, and had been Master of the Wards in the reign of Mary I. The young man told Sir Francis a curious story that he was the illegitimate son of Robert Dudley, Earl of Leicester and Queen Elizabeth. In time the story was relayed by an English agent in Spain to London and officially dismissed as Roman Catholic propaganda aiming to destabilise the Protestant monarchy. Yet there were those who gave it substance.

Arthur Dudley told Sir Francis that he had been brought up by one Robert Southern, servant to Katherine Ashley, then retired governess to Elizabeth. When he was about 5 years old, Dudley said that he entered the care of John Ashley, Katherine's husband, to be educated. It seems, despite official opposition, Dudley enlisted around 1580 as a volunteer to fight in the Netherlands.

In 1583 Arthur Dudley was called back to England as his 'father' Robert Southern was mortally ill. Arriving at Southern's lodgings at Evesham, he was told that Robert Southern was not his father. Southern went on to say that he had been instructed by Katherine Ashley to go to Hampton Court where one of Queen Elizabeth's ladies-in-waiting, Lady Harington, gave him a new-born baby to care for in his household. The infant was said to have been the illegitimate son of an unmarried court lady, who would have been dismissed if the queen had found out about it. The infant was to be brought up as Robert Southern's son and paid for from a source unknown to Southern. Sworn to secrecy on the pain of death Southern knew that he was almost out of reach of execution by mortal hands and his dying legacy to Arthur Dudley was the truth that his parents were the Earl of Leicester and Queen Elizabeth.

Arthur Dudley went on to describe his life to Sir Francis in great detail. If what he said was true it would hand the Roman Catholic opposition of Elizabeth a trump card. Dudley further told Sir Francis that since he had learned of his real parentage he feared for his life and sought exile abroad. Sir Francis understandably had certain doubts about the truth of what he had heard and devised a set of questions that would test Dudley on the relevant events of his life in England, details of the Ashley home and position, and on the main characters mentioned in the story. Dudley replied to all the questions with plausibility. Nevertheless, Sir Francis feared that Arthur Dudley was a credible spy and made an official report to King Philip.

They discussed the possibility that Arthur Dudley's story was a ruse perpetrated by Queen Elizabeth herself to recognise Arthur Dudley as her son to thwart Philip's claim to the English throne. The political ramifications were clear. Philip, too, had instructed his ambassadors to Queen Elizabeth's court to pay particular attention to her health. He monitored her smallpox scare of 1562 when, desperately ill, she commanded her councillors to appoint Robert Dudley Lord Protector should she die. His servant was also given a generous pension of £500; was this to buy his silence as 'doorkeeper' while Dudley and Elizabeth were intimate in her chambers? Diplomatic dispatches arrived regularly in Madrid on the queen's gastro-enteritis, varicose ulcers, various neuroses and migraines. Philip remembered that the Spanish ambassador reported that he had seen the queen to have 'a swollen belly'. It was put about that this was the consequence of ascites (abdominal dropsy) wherein an accumulation of fluid builds up in the belly. What if, mused Philip, this had been a cover-up for pregnancy?

The king now advised that the best course of action was to hold Arthur Dudley in secure quarters in a monastery pending further investigation. State papers in Spain have only confirmed that this is what happened to Dudley, who seems to have been kept in some comfort. From this point the trail goes cold for historians; was Arthur Dudley kept there for the rest of his life? Did he ever return to England? No one knows, so the Arthur Dudley story can add nothing to the examination of Elizabeth's claim of virginity.

The Burghley State Papers have offered historians a glimpse of what some deduce as a threat to Elizabeth's virginity when she was 15. The noted perpetrator was ambitious malcontent the Lord Admiral Thomas Seymour, Baron Seymour of Sudeley (*c.* 1508–49). He secretly married Queen Dowager Catherine Parr in April 1547, the sixth wife of Henry VIII. Seymour, it should be said, was discontented that his elder brother Edward Seymour, 1st Earl of Hertford and Duke of Somerset had not been more generous towards him. Somerset was Governor and Lord Protector during the boyhood of King Edward VI and had great power in the land. As marrying Mary or Elizabeth was out of the question Seymour saw advantage in marrying Catherine Parr. Now Elizabeth's stepfather, Seymour visited the house in Chelsea where Elizabeth lived with Catherine Parr, and the governess Katherine Ashley, pained by the recollections drawn out of her, recalled:

> Quite often, Seymour would barge into [Elizabeth's] room of a morning before she was ready, and sometimes before she did rise, and if she were up he would bid her good morning and ask how she did, and strike her upon the back or buttocks familiarly ... and sometimes go through to the maidens and play with them, and so forth. And if [Elizabeth] were in her bed he would put open the curtains and bid her good morrow and make as though he would come at her, and she would go further in the bed so that he could not come at her.

Catherine Parr died on 5 September 1548 of puerpal fever and Seymour made attempts to marry Elizabeth; in time Seymour was arrested for treason and imprisoned in the Tower of London in 1549, found guilty and executed.

Reviewing contemporary papers, particularly a dossier prepared during Seymour's treason procedures in which governess Katherine Ashley and Sir Thomas Parry, erstwhile treasurer in Elizabeth's household, were interviewed, modern historians have suggested that Elizabeth may have been sexually abused by Seymour. Projecting a modern analysis on what they see as Seymour's abuse they say that Elizabeth fell in love with Seymour, after all he was something of a court stud; yet that love, they aver, was based on guilt and self-loathing. Psychologically scarred, they go on to say that in adulthood Elizabeth became an abuser, denying (sexual) fulfilment to those she had influence over, from her favourites to her ladies-in-waiting on whom she forced celibacy. Certainly she was hard on any who lapsed. When her maids of honour, Mary Fitton and Anne Vavasour, fell pregnant out of wedlock, for instance, she had the fathers imprisoned and the girls banished from court. Again, when Henry Wriothesley, 3rd Earl of Southampton, secretly married maid of honour Elizabeth Vernon, the queen had them placed in the Fleet prison because her permission had not been sought.

It is well attested that Seymour 'snatched kisses' from Elizabeth, and 'stole embraces' from her while his wife looked on. There was even suggestion of flirtatious horse-play in the bedroom and garden with Catherine Parr present, occasions on which governess Katherine Ashley remonstrated with them. In reply to Ashley's indignation about his dealings with Elizabeth, sometimes dressed only in his nightgown, Seymour said pompously: 'I will tell my Lord Protector [his brother Somerset] how I am slandered; and I will not leave off, for I mean no evil.'

Why Catherine Parr condoned her husband's cavorting with Elizabeth – at times dressed only in his nightshirt – is a matter of speculation. Catherine was a pious woman, whose radical religious writings were admired; eventually she removed Elizabeth to the care of Sir Anthony Denny, MP and counsellor to Edward VI, and his wife Joan, at Cheshunt, Hertfordshire. Before she left Catherine lectured Elizabeth on being careful not to harm her reputation through her conduct. Elizabeth was to admit that (uncharacteristically) she 'answered little' to the reproof. Had the forbidden fruit of sex been tasted? Historian and Elizabeth I biographer Dr David Starkey, writing in 2000, said: 'I think there is good reason to believe that the affair with Seymour was sexual.'

For those who dismiss the theory that Elizabeth lost her virginity to Thomas Seymour, or anyone else, there are always the suppositions concerning Elizabeth's gynaecological history.

As the years of her reign went by, with Elizabeth maintaining her decision not to marry, gossip grew that she had some sexual deficit that made marital relations and reproduction impossible. After her death Elizabeth's godson the wit, author and High Sheriff of Somerset, Sir John Harrington, suggested that she had 'in body some indisposition to the act of marriage'. Dramatist and poet Ben Jonson further gossiped that the queen 'had a membrana on her, which made her incapable of men, though for her delight she tried many'. Again, Elizabeth Talbot, Countess of Shrewsbury, once a lady-in-waiting to Elizabeth, remarked to Mary, Queen of Scots, who was in the care of her husband George, the 6th Earl, at Tutbury, that Elizabeth was 'not like other women' suggesting that she had no periods.

The treatment of the queen's cadaver at death remains uncertain; she left instructions that she should not be embalmed. Medical historians suggest that her death certificate might have included that she died of an infected parotid gland, bronchopneumonia, cancer of the stomach and thyroid failure. It seems that her heart was removed and was purported to be seen in a casket (along with that of her sister Mary) in the vault of George Monck, Duke of

Albemarle, who was interred in the Henry VII Chapel, Westminster Abbey, in 1670 the year of Monck's death.

So despite learned opinion there is no watertight proof that Elizabeth I was not a biological virgin all her life. And for all time she will be known as the 'Virgin Queen'.

Did King Alfred really burn the cakes?

Alfred found learning dead and he restored it
Education neglected and he revived it
The laws powerless and he gave them force
The church debased and he raised it
The land ravaged by a fearful enemy from which he delivered it
Alfred's name will live as long as mankind shall respect the past.

Inscription on the statue of King Alfred (1877)
by Count Gleichen in Wantage town centre.

Alfred the Great, undoubtedly the most widely known of the West Saxons, was born around 847, the fourth son and fifth child of Ethelwulf and his wife Osburh; he was of the house of his grandfather Egbert, first of the great Wessex monarchs. Historians, following the lead of Alfred biographer and chaplain Asser, later Bishop of Sherborne, identify his place of birth as a royal villa, where Wantage now stands, in the Vale of the White Horse, Oxfordshire. Today Alfred remains a character of myth, his life venerated by chroniclers down the ages as the 'saviour of the Saxons' from the onslaughts of the Norsemen.

Alfred grew up in an atmosphere of great religious devotion and made visits to Rome. He is thought to have brought a period of prosperity to England, establishing burghs (defensive strongholds), designing a navy, and as a scholar promoting a written record of his era.

The monk Florence of Worcester (d.1118), wrote this of Alfred in *Chronicon ex Chronicis*:

> Alfred the king of the Anglo-Saxons, the son of the most pious king Ethelwulf, the famous, the warlike, the victorious; the careful provider for the widow, the helpless, the orphan and the poor, the most skilled of Saxon poets, most dear of his own nation, courteous to all, most liberal, endowed with prudence, fortitude, justice and temperance; most patient in the infirmity from which he continually suffered; the most discerning investigator in executing justice, most watchful and devout in the service of god.

Some believe that Alfred actively encouraged monastic scribes to write up the annals known as *The Anglo-Saxon Chronicle*. Certainly the *Chronicle* contains an account of Alfred's battles and forms stirring propaganda for the ruling house of Wessex upon which throne Alfred sat during 871–899. It was Matthew Parris, the thirteenth-century Benedictine monk in his *Historia* who identifies Alfred as the first king to reign over all England, which in Alfred's time meant the land south and west of Roman Watling Street.

Alfred began his rule on 23 April 871 on the death of King Ethelred of battle wounds. In this year Wessex felt the full fury of the Norsemen (Danes), who pushed west up the Thames. They were defeated at the Battle of Ashdown. Nevertheless, Alfred was driven into Somerset to contemplate an effective counter-attack. Here was the scenario of the 'Alfred and the Cakes' story. The actual recorded tale goes like this: When Alfred was fleeing from the Norsemen and before he beat them at the Battle of Edington in 878, he took refuge anonymously in the house of a swineherd and his family. The swineherd's wife left a batch of loaves by the fire next to Alfred who sat sharpening arrows, preoccupied with his military problems. When the woman returned she saw her loaves were smouldering.

Irate she berated Alfred: 'You wretch, you're only too fond of them when they're nicely done. Why can't you turn them when you see them burning?' A chastened Alfred meekly turned the loaves. The swineherd's wife's reaction when she discovered who she had been chastising is not recorded.

Where did the cakes story come from? Biographer Bishop Asser does not mention it, and the earliest traced version is in the anonymous twelfth-century *Life of St Neot*. The ninth-century ex-soldier-cum-monk of Glastonbury Abbey, St Neot is believed to have been a kinsman of Alfred, perhaps even his half-brother, who Alfred consulted on various matters. St Neot was a powerful influence; some of his relics appeared at St Neots, Cambridgeshire, from where St Anslem gave a portion to the Abbey of Bec, Normandy. St Neot's life identifies the location of the swineherd's dwelling as Athelney 'in the remote parts of English Britain far to the west ... surrounded on all sides by vast salt marshes ...' That is the Somerset levels. It was Matthew Parker (d.1575), Queen Elizabeth I's Archbishop of Canterbury, in editing Asser's biography of Alfred, who gave future life to the 'cakes' story.

In 868 Alfred married Ealhswith (d.902), granddaughter of the King of Mercia, and had five children. Three of Alfred's granddaughters became wives of European monarchs, placing Alfred firmly in 'the genealogy of the royal houses of Europe'. By 896 the sinister shadows of the Norsemen had been lifted and Alfred's kingdom entered a period of peace. Alfred probably died at Winchester, 26 October 899, and modern medical historians believe that he suffered from Crohn's Disease, in part an illness of the intestinal tract. Alfred was buried in the Old Minster at Winchester, to be later interred before the high altar of the New Minster; again his cadaver was moved to the royal tombs at Hyde Abbey, a site much despoiled in later years.

The story of Alfred and the cakes has a certain plausibility about it; yet, was it a piece of pro-Alfred propaganda? Perhaps it was to show

how Arthur, the great warrior, could show the spirit of meekness so prized by his devout court. Who knows, but the famous story has probably done more to keep Alfred's memory in the general public eye than his historical activities.

Was King James II/VII's baby son a changeling?

Changeling: A child substituted for another.

Chambers 20th Century Dictionary.

James had caught the first glimpse of a hope which delighted and elated him. The Queen was with child.

Thomas Babington, Baron Macaulay (1800–59),
History *(1848).*

In the early days of 1688, gossip began to flow through the corridors of court to the coffee houses of London that King James II/VII's second wife, Queen Mary of Modena, now married fourteen years, was absenting herself from public ceremonies. The excuse was indisposition. Few were fooled. Her Catholic ladies were hanging sacred relics around her bed for a safe pregnancy with the added prayer that the child be a son. The nation listened to the gossip with a mixture of sarcasm and apprehension.

What was extraordinary about this? Nothing. Although the monarch was 54, his wife was 29 and in full health. Although it was five years since her last pregnancy, she had borne four children, although they had all died young. Many in the nation believed that there would never be an heir to the throne from King James's loins, and considered the gossip to be the beginnings of a Jesuit plot.

King James had turned Roman Catholic in 1668 and his wife Mary was an ardent upholder of the faith. James's Declaration of Indulgence of April 1687, restoring rights to Roman Catholics to service in any administrative position, and the king's determination to overthrow the Church of England, engendered a huge anti-Catholic surge among his largely Protestant subjects. This was made worse when the pregnancy rumours were rife for triumphant Roman Catholics at the prospect of a male Catholic heir stuck in the nation's craw. As Lord Macaulay wrote in his *History*: 'The Roman Catholics would have acted more wisely if they had spoken of the pregnancy as a natural event, and if they had borne with moderation their unexpected good fortune.'

On the morning of Sunday 10 June 1688, Prince James Francis Edward Stuart was born at St James's Palace. Detractors believed that Mary had been moved from Whitehall at dead of night to the less commodious accommodation of St James's to suit nefarious Catholic purposes. For many Protestants, St James's Palace was riddled with Roman Catholic priests 'running disreputable errands along secret passages'. This birthday, though, would be kept sacred by Roman Catholics, but it set in motion another curious rumour. The gossips said that the child had been born dead and that a changeling had been smuggled into the Queen's room in a warming pan to conceal a stillbirth; and that the whole was a Roman Catholic plot. One of the promoters and believers of such a plot was Gilbert Burnet, Bishop of Salisbury, who made much of it in his *History of his own Times* published eight years after his death in 1715.

The ridiculousness of this gossip is self-evident. Purely for political purposes, such a royal birth was a public event in which many courtiers would be present. Estimates show that there were sixty-seven witnesses in the queen's bedchamber, of which eighteen were privy councillors; thus, too many persons to be privy to a conspiracy. Yet, the warming pan story was so disquieting that King James called two extraordinary sessions of his Privy Council to hear testimony that the new Prince of Wales was the son of Queen Mary by him.

Within a few months of Prince James's birth and the public announcement that he would be brought up a Roman Catholic, the coup of Whig aristocrats named the Glorious Revolution erupted, and eventually James II/VII fled his kingdom to permanent exile. The baby would enter history as the 'Old Pretender' giving birth to the movement of the Jacobites and the romance of their activities that lives on today.

If Edward VIII had not abdicated who would be monarch today – and why did the abdication cause a 'royal feud'?

> Hark the Herald Angels sing,
> Mrs Simpson pinched our King.
>
> *Street doggerel at the Abdication, 1936.*

On the death of George V on 20 January 1936, his eldest son Edward Albert Christian George Andrew Patrick David, Prince of Wales, born at White Lodge, Richmond Park, Surrey, 23 June 1894, ascended the throne of Great Britain as HM King Edward VIII. Eleven months later at Windsor Castle he uttered these famous words in a broadcast to the nation: '… you must believe me when I tell you that I have found it impossible to carry out the heavy burden of responsibility and to discharge my duties as King as I would wish to do without the help and support of the woman I love.'

A few minutes after 2 p.m., on Saturday 12 December 1936, two days after signing the Instrument of Abdication, the king left

England aboard HMS *Fury* bound for France. He was now HRH the Duke of Windsor. On 3 June 1937 the Duke of Windsor married the 41-year-old twice-divorced American, Mrs Wallis Warfield Simpson, at the house lent by Charles Bedaux, the Château de Candé in Touraine, France. A civil ceremony had been conducted by the Mayor of Monts, docteur Mercier, followed by a religious service celebrated by the Revd Robert Anderson Jardine, vicar of St Paul's church, Darlington (who had volunteered to marry the royal couple in defiance of his bishop's order not to). Thereafter, the Duke and Duchess of Windsor entered exile until the duke's death on 28 May 1972.

When Edward VIII had become king, his brother Prince Albert, Duke of York became heir presumptive. He was not heir apparent because there was no reason why the 42-year-old king would not have children on marriage. If Edward had still been on the throne in 1952, when his brother Prince Albert (who became King George VI on Edward's abdication) died, and if Edward had had no children, then Princess Elizabeth (the present Queen Elizabeth II), Prince Albert's elder daughter would have become heir presumptive. What of Edward's other brothers? The bisexual Prince George, Duke of Kent, had died in 1942, and the next male brother after Prince Albert, Prince Henry, Duke of Gloucester, would not have become heir presumptive unless Princess Elizabeth and Princess Margaret had predeceased him. So Princess Elizabeth would have become Queen Elizabeth II on Edward's death in 1972 instead of ascending the throne in 1952.

The abdication had several other consequences for the Royal Family. On the one hand the entry of Wallis Simpson, as one historian put it, 'was to act as a catalyst in the removal of a disastrously unsuitable monarch from the British throne'; and on the other it produced an on-going 'royal feud' between the Duchess of Windsor and the new queen who eventually became Queen Elizabeth, the Queen Mother. The use of the term 'feud' in this connection seems to have originated with the Duchess of Windsor. For some thirty years the two women never met but when George VI died at the age of only 56, psychologically worn out by the stress of monarchy, the widowed Queen Mother referred to the Duchess of Windsor as 'the woman who killed my husband'. History records that the Duchess of Windsor's description of the Queen Mother ranged from the 'Dowdy Duchess' to 'the Monster of Glamis'.

Out of all of Edward VIII's sisters-in-law, Queen Elizabeth, then Duchess of York, was the closest and most supportive. All that changed when Wallis Simpson arrived in his life in 1931. Apart from his devastated mother, and his puzzled sister the Princess Royal, Elizabeth had many reasons to regret the abdication. In the first place a huge lifelong burden would pass to her shy, stuttering husband who had not been trained like his brother for monarchy; there would be stress for herself too, as now a whole new complexity entered the royal equation. Elizabeth genuinely admired Edward VIII, sustained him when he was having difficulties with his father George V, and often sought to raise his spirits.

Edward VIII – dubbed Duke of Windsor after the abdication – believed that after he sojourned in Europe for a while and after his marriage to Wallis Simpson, he could return to Britain, live at his beloved Fort Belvedere, and reinvent a role for himself (on his own terms), with his new wife at his side; a wife accepted, of course, by the Royal Family as 'Her Royal Highness'. None of this happened. It is still widely believed that the Duchess of Windsor was denied the HRH title because of Queen Elizabeth's influence over her husband.

It was said too, that driven by hatred of the Duchess of Windsor, Queen Elizabeth was completely hostile to the Windsors. Historians feel that this is an unjust view. What Queen Elizabeth resented was what the Windsors were doing to her husband. For some considerable time the Duke of Windsor showered his brother George VI with unwelcome advice, demands, complaints about perceived snubs to himself and his wife, and bullying. Wherever they went in Europe they were an embarrassment to the Royal Family back home. All of which, in particular, made Queen Elizabeth nervous about their future effect on her husband. Should the Windsors come back to Britain, Elizabeth was afraid they would upstage the Royal Family in social circles. The Windsors did return to Britain in September 1939 as guests of Maj Edward and Lady Alexandra Metcalfe, but the duchess was not received by the Royal Family, and the duke only saw the king. In Columbia University, New York, in an archive of papers of Prince Paul of Yugoslavia, there is a letter dated 2 October 1939 which makes Queen Elizabeth's views on the Windsors quite clear:

> I had taken the precaution to send [the Duchess of Windsor] a message before they came [as the Metcalfe's guests] saying that I was sorry that I could not receive her. I thought it more honest to make things quite clear. So she kept away, & nobody saw her. What a curse black sheep are in a family.

Wallis Simpson, the duchess, had met Elizabeth for the first time at Buckingham Palace on 27 November 1934. Commenting in 1974, the Dowager Lady Hardinge of Penhurst remembered this of the encounter:

> I am afraid Mrs Simpson went down badly with [Elizabeth] from the word go. It may have been rather ostentatious dress, or the fact that she allowed the Prince of Wales to push her forward in what seemed an inappropriate manner. The Duchess of York was never discourteous in my experience, but those of us who knew her well could always tell when she did not care for something or someone, and it was very apparent to me that she did not care for Mrs Simpson at all.

Later Wallis Simpson mimicked Elizabeth's 'voice, mannerisms and facial expressions' during a party at Fort Belvedere. Elizabeth walked in as Mrs Simpson was giving her performance and one guest, Ella Hogg, noted: '… from the moment of overhearing, the Duchess of York became her implacable enemy. Mrs Simpson said she had no sense of humour.'

Queen Elizabeth certainly disliked the Duchess of Windsor's 'indiscretions' as she saw it, and her 'proprietory manner with Edward VIII'. Perhaps the Duchess of Windsor's bitterness at the perceived ill-treatment of her husband by his family outweighed any feelings she had for Queen Elizabeth. Overall both women were strong, determined characters, vital, energetic and fun loving; and both dominated their husbands; as well as being 'cheerfully fond of alcohol'. The Duchess of Windsor was once asked: 'Why the feud?' She replied that she believed Queen Elizabeth was jealous of her for marrying Edward VIII instead of him marrying her.

Pretenders, Usurpers and Romances

Was Lady Jane Grey a rightful queen or a child victim?

Oh, Merciful God, consider my misery, best known unto Thee; and be Thou unto me a strong tower of defence. I humbly require Thee. Suffer me not to be tempted above my power, but either be Thou a deliverer unto me out of this great misery, or else give me grace patiently to bear Thy heavy hand and sharp correction ...

Plea of Lady Jane Grey penned at the Tower of London,
11 February 1554.

Known to history as 'the Nine Days Queen', Jane Grey was the blameless sacrifice in the plots of her zealous father-in-law John Dudley, Duke of Northumberland. He endeavoured to hold the Protestant religion in sway in England following the death of the young King Edward VI in 1553, instead of the Roman Catholic dominance which would result from the crowning of Henry VIII's eldest daughter Mary. How did the 15-year-old Lady Jane Grey fall foul of England's vicious Tudor politics?

Born at Bradgate Manor, 5 miles from the market town of Leicester, on or around 12 October 1537 – the same day that Prince Edward, Henry VIII's only male heir was born – Jane Grey was the granddaughter of Princess Mary Tudor, Queen of France and Duchess of Suffolk, sister of Henry VIII; Jane was the eldest daughter of Henry and Frances Grey, later Duke and Duchess of Suffolk. Diminutive in stature yet admired for her beauty and sweetness of character, as great-niece of Henry VIII Jane was prominently placed in society and very well-educated for the day. She spent her childhood at Bradgate and the Grey's Westminster home at Dorset Place. A classics scholar with a great talent for languages and a staunch adherent of the Protestant Reformation, Jane's father's chaplain John Aylmer (d.1594), later Bishop of London, acted as her tutor. In 1546 Jane became a member of the household of Queen Catherine Parr, a close friend of her grandmother now Dowager Duchess of Suffolk. Jane's life at Queen Catherine's Chelsea Manor House, the royal court, and later the Seymour home of Sudeley Castle, Gloucestershire, when Catherine married once more, brought Jane into contact with the highest in the land. Her happy life was disrupted on the early morning of 6 September 1548, when the 36-year-old Catherine Parr died of childbirth fever, whereupon Jane became the ward of Queen Catherine's second husband Lord High Admiral, Sir Thomas Seymour, Lord Sudeley, brother of Edward, Duke of Somerset, Lord Protector of England during the minority of Edward VI.

From this point Lady Jane Grey became a political pawn. Her fate developed in this way: During his last days Edward VI signed an amendment to his late father's 1546 will – the ambiguous *Device* – setting out a new succession path for the English throne. In its hastily drafted wording Edward's half-sisters Mary and Elizabeth would not succeed him, or the descendant of his aunt Margaret, Queen of Scots. Instead the male heirs of Lady Frances (Grey), Duchess of Suffolk and niece of Henry VIII, would succeed. As there were none at this date this meant that the male heirs of Frances's surviving daughters Jane, Catherine and Mary would succeed. When the amendment was written the girls had no sons, so the Privy Council directed that the throne should go to Lady Jane Grey as heiress presumptive. There was some doubt among the Privy Councillors of the legality of the *Device* but on Edward VI's death on 6 July 1553, Jane was duly named successor and proclaimed Queen of England in London on 10 July. Jane did not want to become queen and made this disavowal: 'The Crown is not my right, and pleaseth me not. The Lady Mary is the rightful heir.' Nevertheless, she was persuaded that her ascension to the throne would help the Protestant cause. Meanwhile, Henry VIII's eldest daughter Mary, favoured successor to her half-brother, particularly by Roman Catholic interests, fled to East Anglia to muster loyal forces to her cause.

A few weeks before the succession, on 21 May 1553, Jane Grey married largely for political reasons. She wed Lord Guildford Dudley, the 17-year-old sixth son of the 1st Duke of Northumberland at Durham House, London. The marriage was against her will and Jane was coerced into it by intimidation and violence.

The Duke of Northumberland had assumed the role of Protector of the Realm during Edward VI's reign. His scheme was to have his son declared joint-monarch with Jane. This, Jane refused to countenance, for at the beginning of her marriage she had little affection for her husband. The English nobility were unhappy with Northumberland's schemes and in the country there was growing support for Mary Tudor. Jane Grey held the title of Queen of England for nine days, 10–19 July 1553, for Northumberland's supporting army was dispersed without bloodshed and he was arrested and beheaded for treason on 22 August 1553. Jane Grey and her husband were arrested too, and imprisoned in the Tower.

At first Mary Tudor, who was crowned queen at Westminster Abbey on 1 October 1553, was prepared to be lenient to the teenage 'usurper' to her throne. But two factors brought Jane's ultimate doom nearer. Her father Henry Grey was involved in the rebellion against Queen Mary organised by Sir Thomas Wyatt and Edward Courtney, Earl of Devonshire to prevent the marriage of Mary to the Roman Catholic King Philip of Spain. Again, Jane Grey refused to recant her Protestantism.

Jane was found guilty of treason at the Guildhall, London. The sentence was death, but as Jane was of royal blood her execution had to be observed reverently. She was led to the block by Lieutenant of the Tower of London, Sir John Brydges, and accompanied by 200 Yeomen of the Guard. Witnesses said that she met her end with 'calm fortitude', yet when blindfolded she showed anxiety when she could not locate 'the block with her grasping hands'; thus aged 16 Lady Jane Grey died on Tower Green on 12 February 1554. A little earlier the same day Jane's husband was executed on the same charge at Tower Hill; a more public location. From the window of her prison Jane watched his headless body being borne away on a cart. Jane was buried without religious ceremony alongside her husband near the north wall of the chancel of the Chapel Royal of St Peter ad Vincula in the Tower, not far from the bodies of executed queens Anne Boleyn and Catherine Howard. A modern representative of Lady Jane Grey through her sister Catherine, wife of Edward Seymour, Earl of Hertford, is Beatrice Mary Grenville Morgan-Grenville, Lady Kinloss (b.1922). According to the will of Henry VIII her line has a legitimate line to the throne.

Who was England's 'Lost Queen'?

How do I thank thee, Death, and bless thy power
That I have passed the guard and 'scaped the Tower!
And now my pardon is my epitaph
And a small coffin my poor carcase hath;
For at thy charge both soul and body were
Enlarged at last, secure from hope and fear
That among saints, this among kings is laid,
And what my birth did claim my death has paid.

Lines by the Bishop of Norwich at the death of
Lady Arbella Stuart.

Look down the family tree of Lady Arbella Stuart and her name appears boldly among the dynasties of the Tudors and Stuarts. See how the spider's web of branches trace her back to her great-great-grandfather Henry VII of England, down through her great-grandmother Margaret, Queen of Scots, her grandmother Margaret, wife of Matthew Stuart, 4th Earl of Lennox, to her father Charles Stuart, 6th Earl of Lennox (d.1576) and mother Elizabeth Cavendish (d.1581), brother and sister-in-law of Henry Stuart, Lord Darnley, second husband of Mary, Queen of Scots. There Arbella's name sits alongside her husband William Seymour, who in time became Duke of Somerset, who could also trace his lineage back through Mary, daughter of Henry VII. Together they made a dangerous dynastic threat to others seeking the throne.

Arbella Stuart (Latinised: Arabella) was born around 10 November 1575 at the Hackney house of her paternal grandmother Margaret, Lady Lennox, and christened at the parish church of Chatsworth. Charles Stuart, her father, died when Arbella was 18 months old, leaving her mother Elizabeth in strained financial circumstances. Elizabeth died when Arbella was 6 and the child was now in the charge of her grandmother, four times married Elizabeth Talbot, Countess of Shrewsbury, known to history as the redoubtable, ambitious 'Bess of Hardwick'. Well-educated, and because of her background, Arbella knew well the courts of Elizabeth I – who thought her pushy and arrogant – and James I/VI. To James she was an unsettling figure; she was after all James's first cousin and to many Arbella had a more legitimate right to the throne than James on the death of Queen Elizabeth in 1603. James was the senior descendant of Henry VII, but had not Henry VIII's will declared that all 'aliens' be excluded from the succession? Born in Scotland in 1566 James was considered by some as an 'alien', but Arbella being English-born was not an alien in these terms. Thus, to James's supporters Arbella was a dynastic threat.

In the early months of his reign James ignored the tortuous rumours that linked Arbella with alleged plotting against him by such men as Henry Brook, 8th Lord Cobham and Sir Walter Raleigh. Their scheme was to depose James and put Arbella on the throne; their machinations earned them a capital sentence which James countermanded in his own idiosyncratic way at the last minute. Until 1609 James then treated Arbella with kindness yet parsimony. He kept her at court where he could keep an eye on her. But alas, her marriage caused her to descend into disaster.

Over the years Arbella's name was linked for future matrimony 'with every single prince in Christendom'. Yet her romance with William Seymour is somewhat lacking in historic detail. By 2 February 1610 they were betrothed and married on 21 June. Arbella's marriage to Seymour was provocative to King James; it had been in secret and without the permission of her royal cousin. This act of 'virtual treason' to a man twelve years her junior had sent King James into a frenzied fit. Not only was a royal prerogative slighted, but Seymour was a dynastic threat, for he was a grandson of Lady Catherine Grey who was of the line descending from Margaret Tudor. So for her secret marriage James put William Seymour in the Tower and Arbella under house arrest at Lambeth with plans to move her out of harms way to the north of England under the supervision of the Bishop of Durham. En route for Durham, Arbella fell ill (or pretended to be so), and the party lodged at a 'sorry inn'. From here, on 3 June 1611, dressed as a man, she slipped away from her captors, for both she and her husband had planned a double yet separate escape. William effected a successful escape but was delayed by a rapid hue-and-cry from making rendezvous with Arbella. Incandescent with rage King James ordered the Lord High Admiral, the Earl of Nottingham, to organise a pursuit as the escapees made their separate ways to France. The pursuit was carried out by Admiral Sir William Monson. Arbella's party was able to join Captain Corvé's French barque to take them to France, however, just off Calais Arbella was caught by Captain Griffen Cockett's pinnace *Adventure* and she was returned to England. William Seymour successfully escaped to Ostend. In time he made his peace with James and received the Garter and the dukedom of Somerset in the year of his death, 1660.

After capture James incarcerated Arbella in the Tower as a 'close prisoner' under the Lieutenant of the Tower Sir William Waad (or Wade). Although in close confinement she was allowed servants. Her health declined and she was reported to be 'dangerously sick of convulsions' to which was added that she 'continues crakt in her brain'. Plots flowed round her for her escape but they came to nothing. At length she died on 25 September 1615; some said she had been poisoned, but she is more likely to have died from malnutrition. In death she had a little more honour, although King James ordered that there be no court mourning for his royal cousin. James further ordered that her coffin be laid inside the tomb which he had constructed for his mother Mary, Queen of Scots, whose cadaver was moved from Peterborough Cathedral to Westminster Abbey. This is a strange quirk of fate: When Mary Stuart fled to England after her deposition, one of her successive custodians was

Bess of Hardwick at the Shrewsbury family country houses of Sheffield Castle, Sheffield Lodge and Chatsworth. There Arbella, Mary Stuart's niece-in-law, had been her child companion.

There is some doubt among historians whether or not Arbella had any pretensions to the throne of England and Scotland, despite the possible brainwashing to this end by her maternal grandmother Bess of Hardwick. So Arbella Stuart has lain in Westminster Abbey scarcely noticed yet had she been male, she might have succeeded to the throne after all.

Why did Henry VIII marry six times?

Choose yourself a wife you will always and only love.

> *Advice of John Skelton (c. 1460–1529), created poet laureate by Oxford and Cambridge universities, to pupil Prince Henry (later Henry VIII), in 'Speculum Principis', (c. 1499).*

Henry VIII's marriage records read like this:

1. Catherine of Aragon (1485–1536), daughter of Ferdinand II, King of Aragon and Isabel I, Queen of Castile, married at Greyfriars church, Greenwich, 11 June 1509. Marriage annulled, 23 May 1533. Six children; only one survived, became Queen Mary I.

2. Anne (*c.* 1500–36), daughter of Thomas Boleyn, Earl of Wiltshire and Ormonde and Lady Elizabeth Howard, married at York Place (later Whitehall Palace), 25 January 1533. Marriage declared invalid, 17 May 1536. Executed. Three children; one ruled as Elizabeth I.

3. Jane (*c.* 1508–37), daughter of Sir John Seymour and Margery Wentworth, married at Whitehall Palace, 30 May 1536. Died in childbirth. Son became King Edward VI.

4. Anne (1515–57), daughter of Johann II, Duke of Cleves and Marie of Julich and Berg, married at Greenwich Palace, 6 January 1540. Marriage annulled, 9 July 1540. No offspring.

5. Catherine (*c.* 1520–42), daughter of Lord Henry Howard and first wife Joyce Culpeper, married at Oatlands Park, Surrey, 28 July 1540. Executed. No offspring.

6. Catherine (*c.* 1512–48), daughter of Sir Thomas Parr of Kendal and Maud Green, married at Hampton Court Palace, 12 July 1543. Outlived Henry to marry again. No offspring.

Although Catherine of Aragon became Henry VIII's first queen she was first married to his brother Arthur, Prince of Wales, on 14 November 1501. Five months after the marriage, the consumptive, syphilitic Arthur died at Ludlow Castle. Had the marriage been consummated – 'last night I was in Spain', boasted Arthur – did he infect his wife with syphilis? These were to remain mysteries to be raked over later, for Catherine insisted that she came out of her first marriage *virgo intacta*.

By 1503 Catherine was proposed as a bride for Prince Henry; a papal dispensation was obtained from Pope Julius II for Henry to marry his brother's widow, yet Henry VII dithered in pressing for the marriage ceremony as he hoped for a better candidate for Henry's nuptial bed. No such candidate appeared, and on the death of Henry VII in 1509, Henry, ardently in love, married Catherine at Greyfriar's church, Greenwich on 11 June. Four children were born; three stillborn and one who lived barely eight weeks, until in 1516 Catherine gave birth to Mary Tudor. Another stillborn birth occurred in 1518, following two further miscarriages. Catherine had no more pregnancies.

Henry and Catherine ceased to co-habit in 1526 and the following year the long divorce process began. The basis of Henry's divorce suit was affinity; that is it was 'illegal' for him to marry his brother's widow despite the Pope's dispensation. Although Catherine had powerful support from her nephew, the Emperor Charles V, and in Rome, a compliant Thomas Cranmer, Archbishop of Canterbury, declared the marriage null and void on 23 May 1533 and an Act of Parliament sealed the issue.

Catherine was demoted to Dowager Princess of Wales. Throughout she refused to accept the divorce and died of cancer at Kimbolton Castle on 7 January 1536. The queen Henry had loved with a deep devotion and whose spirit was never crushed by the divorce was buried at Peterborough Cathedral.

Contemporary commentators suggest that Henry also fell in love with his second wife Anne Boleyn. Anne knew the ramifications of court life well. Her father held various diplomatic posts and she served as a court lady in the household of Henry VIII's sister Mary, Queen of France, then that of King Louis XII of France's daughter Claude, and by 1521 she was back in England as maid of honour to Queen Catherine of Aragon.

Anne's French court manners were considered charming by the young gentlemen at Henry VIII's court. Records show that she had a probable sexual relationship with Henry Percy, son of the Earl of Northumberland, then resident in the household of Cardinal Wolsey. It is likely too that they had some sort of betrothal agreement. Her name was also linked with the notorious adulterer Sir Thomas Wyatt, whose pursuit of Anne would later earn him a sojourn in the Tower. Henry VIII paid her increasing attention too, transferring his affection from his mistress, Anne's elder sister Mary Boleyn. For some time Anne fended off Henry's advances, but kept him interested with coquettish flirting and amorous letters. Probably she became his mistress around 1527 and in 1532 Henry made her Marchioness of Pembroke. Anne was pregnant by Henry in December 1532, and at that point a divorce from Catherine of Aragon loomed prominently in Henry's mind.

The divorce was sealed by parliament in May 1533, but Anne and Henry had been secretly married on 25 January that year; five days after the divorce Anne was crowned queen, the last queen consort ever to have a separate coronation. Anne gave birth to Princess Elizabeth on 7 September and Henry's disappointment at not having a son meant his ardour for Anne diminished. By 1534 he had taken up with one of Anne's ladies-in-waiting, Jane Seymour.

The loss of a possible male heir by miscarriage in 1536 brought Anne's fate nearer. A commission was set up to examine her conduct. In time, on no real evidence and dubious accusations extracted by torture, Anne was accused of an incestuous relationship with her brother George, Viscount Rochford, and treasonous adultery with a gentleman of the King's Chamber, Henry Norris. The superstitious, too, noted that the deformity on one of her hands (a rudimentary sixth finger) indicated that she was a witch. Anne was arrested and taken to the Tower where she was interrogated about her life and relationships. On 17 May 1536 an ecclesiastical court declared the royal marriage null and void *ab initio* (from the beginning); again the pretext of affinity was quoted because of Henry's relationship with Mary Boleyn.

Anne was condemned to death and beheaded on Tower Green on 19 May 1536, to be buried at the Chapel of St Peter ad Vincula. Just before her death Anne summed up her royal progress: 'The king has been very good to me. He promoted me from a simple maid to be a marchioness. Then he raised me to be a queen. Now he will raise me to be a martyr.'

A day after the execution of Anne Boleyn, Henry announced his betrothal to Jane Seymour and they were married eleven days later. Jane Seymour was half second-cousin to Anne Boleyn so she was not out of place as maid of honour to Catherine of Aragon and Anne Boleyn, despite her somewhat humble birth as daughter of a 'simple knight', Sir John Seymour of Nettlestead, Suffolk. Jane was not considered a court beauty and her skills were not to promote any physical attributes but to entrap Henry VIII. She seduced him by posing as a simple, innocent girl. Courtiers noted that she successfully resisted Henry's carnal approaches with the inference that the road to her bed was through marriage; she was after all a conservative Roman Catholic.

When Anne Boleyn was being tried and executed Jane Seymour with discretion took up residence at the family house of Wolf Hall, near Savernake, Wiltshire. Eleven days after Anne's execution Henry and Jane were married in the Queen's Closet, York Place. The outbreak of plague in London and Jane's pregnancy meant that plans for Jane's coronation were put off (she was never crowned). On 12 October 1537 Jane gave birth to a boy, Prince Edward, at Hampton Court. Henry was ecstatic and ordered lavish celebrations; his son's christening was attended by both his half-sisters, Mary and Elizabeth. Twelve days after the birth Jane died of puerperal fever and she was buried in St George's chapel, Windsor. As herald and chronicler Charles Wriothesley (d.1562) commented, Jane 'reigned as the King's wife ... one year and a quarter'. She had given Henry what he most desired, a son, and for him she was the 'perfect wife'. How long Jane would have remained in Henry's favour after Edward's birth is a matter of speculation.

Jane Seymour was only dead a week when Lord Great Chamberlain, Thomas Cromwell, pressed Henry to seek a wife that would stress an alliance with a foreign royal house. English ambassadors to the Continental courts began their search and by 1538 the daughter of the Duke of Cleves entered the frame. After all, the duke was one of the most keen and strong supporters of the Protestant Reformation. What did she look like? Henry dispatched Hans Holbein to paint a likeness. Henry's envoys backed up the opinion that Anne of Cleves was beautiful 'as the golden sun excelleth the silver moon'.

A marriage negotiation was completed on 4 October 1539 and Dutch-speaking Anne arrived at Deal that December to make for

Rochester to meet her eager fiancé. Henry was aghast at what he saw, dubbing her the 'Flanders Mare', her looks repulsing him. If he could have reneged on the marriage Henry would have gladly. He could not, and the marriage, conducted by Thomas Cranmer, Archbishop of Canterbury, went ahead. The marriage was never consummated – they are said to have played cards on their wedding night for eight hours. A girl of limited education and no knowledge of spoken English, her personality at odds with what Henry found attractive in a woman, forced Henry to eject her from Court. Henry hurried to gather pretexts for an annulment. He had not wanted the marriage; it was not consummated; and had not Anne been pre-contracted to the son of the Duke of Lorraine? That was enough. A convocation pronounced the marriage null and void on 9 July 1540.

Anne did not object to the divorce proceedings. Henry endowed her with money and two houses. A friendship developed between them – he dubbed her 'sister' – and she remained on good terms with her step-children. So Anne became a well-provided divorcee, but some historians believe that she hankered after re-marrying Henry, especially after Catherine Howard was executed. It was not to be and Anne outlived Henry by ten years. Anne died at Chelsea on 17 July 1557. She was buried in a tomb on the south side of the altar of the Confessor's Shrine at Westminster Abbey.

Henry's fifth wife, Catherine Howard, was Anne Boleyn's first cousin, mirroring her sensuality but outdoing her in promiscuity. With her grandfather, the 2nd Duke of Norfolk, Catherine was well placed in court circles, but this highly sexed girl had a long list of physical lovers, from Henry Manox her music teacher, to her cousin Thomas Culpeper. She first met Henry VIII at the London residence of Stephen Gardiner, Bishop of Winchester. Instantly attracted, Henry had Catherine promoted to maid of honour to Anne of Cleves.

Henry's repugnance for Anne of Cleves made it easier for Catherine Howard to ensnare Henry. On that day in May 1540 which marked the annulment of Henry's marriage to Anne of Cleves, the Council urged Henry to move swiftly towards a new marriage 'to the comfort of his realm'. Catherine was well placed through scheming to be prime candidate and Henry and Catherine were married on 28 July 1540.

Refreshed in vitality by his high-spirited bride, Henry rode and hunted with new vigour, and lavished property and jewellery on Catherine. Repulsed by Henry's growing girth and physical ailments, Catherine made the very unwise move of taking up again with her former lovers, particularly one of her grandmother's retainers Francis Dereham and Thomas Culpeper. During a progress that Henry and Catherine made to the northern lands of his kingdom, and with the help of her lady-in-waiting Viscountess Rochford, Catherine had Culpeper smuggled into her apartments. It was only to be expected that Henry would find out when the Council heard of the infidelities. At first Henry did not believe the accusations but, being very upset, he went off on a prolonged hunting trip.

In due time Catherine was placed under house arrest at Syon House, and her lovers along with sundry members of the Howard family were brought to trial. Dereham and Culpeper were executed. In 1542 parliament agreed a Bill of Attainder against Catherine which was given the Royal Assent through the Council (to spare Henry's tender feelings on the matter) on 11 February. Two days later Catherine and her aider and abetter Viscountess Rockford were executed at Tower Green. Catherine was buried near to her cousin Anne Boleyn in the Chapel of St Peter ad Vincula.

Courtiers noted how the infidelities aged Henry VIII further and for a while he was a broken man. At length his spirits revived and a year later he was jockeying again in the marriage stakes. Henry's sixth and last wife Catherine Parr came from a rich, influential northern family which was at the centre of court affairs. Henry VIII was in fact her third husband, she having first married Sir Edward Borough (d. *c.* 1533), and then John Neville, 3rd Baron Latimer (d.1543). Four months after Latimer's death she married Henry at Hampton Court Palace on 12 July 1543.

This time the syphilitic, ailing Henry VIII was looking for a step-mother to his children; from her two marriages Catherine Parr had no children, except step-children from Lord Latimer's first marriage. But in his courtship Henry had a rival. It was gossiped at court that Catherine Parr was enamoured of Henry's brother-in-law Thomas Seymour. Before they could marry Henry intervened and claimed Catherine Parr for himself.

Historically the well-educated 'religious radical', Catherine Parr could be called the first Protestant Queen of England, remembering though, as with Anne of Cleves and Catherine Howard, no arrangements were ever made for her coronation. An accomplished religious debater, Catherine wrote learned papers. This would lead her into danger with the pro-Roman Catholic factions, led by Gardiner and Wriothesley; in 1546 a charge of heresy against her was prepared, although slipping into senility, Henry defended her against the caucus.

Henry's motives for marrying Catherine Parr paid off; she was a kindly, attentive step-mother, bringing together Henry's three mismatched children Mary, Elizabeth and Edward, promoting their education and encouraging their intellectual talents. Catherine gave Henry a round of family life he had not had since Jane Seymour's day. When Henry departed for the war zone in France in 1544 he left Catherine to rule as Governor of the Realm and Protector, a role she carried out with assiduity and competence.

After Henry died at Whitehall, 28 January 1547, Queen Dowager Catherine married the womaniser Thomas Seymour, and became aunt to her step-son now Edward VI. At the age of 36 Catherine became pregnant and gave birth to a daughter. She died of puerperal fever on September 1548, to be buried in St Mary's church,

Sudeley Castle, Gloucestershire. (She was reburied in the Chandos vault in 1817.)

Was George III a bigamist?

All descendants of George II under 25 years of age (except the issue of princesses marrying into foreign families) must obtain royal consent, otherwise the marriage is void.

Royal Marriages Act, 1772.

In the National Archives at Kew there is a curious royal marriage certificate. It enters the name of Prince George William Frederick, Prince of Wales, and a Quaker girl called Hannah Lightfoot, and their marriage as being on 17 April 1759. Officially the prince, who became George III on the death of his grandfather George II in 1760, married at St James's Palace, 8 September 1761, HSH Princess Sophia Charlotte of Mecklenburg Strelitz. So does the Kew certificate show that George III was a bigamist?

Prince George, the son of Frederick Louis, Prince of Wales (d.1751), was born at Norfolk House, London, on 24 May 1738. He was not wayward like his father and despite being obstinate he was well-educated, but among his character faults was a lack of judgement which led him to stuff a skeleton into his juvenile cupboard.

The skeleton was given a public airing in 1866 in the Court of Probate and Divorce, wherein barrister Dr Walter Smith represented one 'Princess' Lavinia, who claimed to be the 'legitimate granddaughter of Prince Henry Frederick, Duke of Cumberland', sixth child of Prince Frederick Louis and George III's brother. The claim, opposed in court by Attorney General Roundell Palmer, and before Lord Chief Justice Sir Alexander Cockburn, was that Lavinia's grandmother Olive Wilmot had secretly married the scapegrace

Cumberland. Lavinia thus pursued recognition of her royal rights and titles in court. The basis of the plaintiff's case was a cache of documents left by Olive Wilmot when she died in 1834. They showed signatures of George III, William Pitt (as Earl of Chatham) and Lord Brooke (as Earl of Warwick) attesting to Olive's royal birth and affirming a clutch of monetary donations to her. In the event the claim was dismissed on a jury verdict, although Lavinia pursued the claim until her death in 1871. During his address to the court barrister Smith made the astonishing claim that before his marriage to Princess Sophia Charlotte, George III had been married to one Hannah Lightfoot. He was queried by the Lord Chief Justice as to the relevance of his statement and was admonished for his 'great indecency to make such uncouth and unverified statements about the royal family'. Yet, the public were intrigued by the assertion: Who was Hannah Lightfoot?

Records show that she was born in London on 12 October 1730, the daughter of Quaker Matthew Lightfoot (d.1733), a shoemaker of Execution Dock, Wapping-in-the-East, and his wife Mary Wheeler (d.1760). Gossip of the day recounts that Prince George first saw Hannah sitting in the window of her uncle's linen draper's shop by St James's Market (now Waterloo Place and Regent Street). Struck by the girl's beauty, he arranged for one of his mother Augusta, Princess of Wales's maids of honour, Elizabeth Chudleigh (later Countess of Bristol), to effect a meeting; this she did, added the court gossips with relish, with the assistance of a high-class pimp called Jack Emm.

When Prince George's father died in 1751 he became heir apparent and it was thought necessary by his mother and others that George's mistress be married. Thus Hannah married a grocer, one Isaac Axelford on 11 December 1753. Other versions of the story say that Prince George snatched Hannah before she could be married to Axford and married her himself in 1757 or 1759; the dates vary from version to version. The documents of the 1866 trial showed that three children were born of the union to be named as George Rex, John Mackleon and Sarah Dalton. The event of children became an accepted story in the biography *The Fair Quaker, Hannah Lightfoot* by Mary Lucy Pendreth. Again, the theme was taken up by John Lindsay in *The Lovely Quaker* who gave further details of George Rex's pedigree and his ultimate residence at the Cape of Good Hope. Professor Ian R. Christie, a historian with a special interest in George III's life and reign, researched the George Rex story with the conclusion that it was 'based on evidence which is without exception hearsay or else suspicious in origin ...' Over the years variations of the Hannah Lightfoot story have emerged, but most note that she died around 1759.

The documents produced for the 1866 trial were deemed a forgery, and today authenticity has never been proven. During the purported year of Hannah Lightfoot's death, Prince George fell in love with Lady Sarah Lennox (1745–1820), daughter of Charles, 2nd Duke of Richmond, a great-granddaughter of Charles II and his mistress Louise de Kéroüalle, Duchess of Portsmouth. The royal family and their advisers thought a marriage for Prince George with a British commoner was not acceptable and a German princess was sought. Thus historians largely agree that if Hannah Lightfoot existed at all there was no marriage between her and Prince George and consequently George III was not a bigamist. However, curious stories persist. Archaeologists working at St Peter's church, Carmarthen, West Wales, in 2000, discovered an unmarked brick barrel vault in the centre of the chancel, before the altar. The work was precipitated by the fact that the huge church organ was sinking and the floor needed shoring up. The organ had been a personal gift, tradition has it, from George III in 1796, who had intended it for Windsor Castle. As the archaeologists worked downwards four coffins were revealed, along with this obscured gravestone:

IN THIS VAULT ARE DEPOSITED THE REMAINS OF
CHARLOTTE AUGUSTA CATHERINE DALTON, ELDEST
DAUGHTER OF JAMES DALTON ESQUIRE, FORMERLY OF
THIS TOWN AND OF BANGALORE IN THE EAST INDIES. SHE
DIED ON THE 2ND DAY OF AUGUST, 1832, AGED 27 YEARS.

ALSO THE REMAINS OF MARGARET AUGUSTA DALTON,
SECOND DAUGHTER OF DANIEL PRYTHERCH, ESQ. OF
THIS TOWN AND OF ABERGOYLE IN THIS COUNTY, BY
CAROLINE HIS WIFE, YOUNGEST DAUGHTER OF THE
ABOVE JAMES DALTON. SHE DIED ON THE 24TH DAY OF
JANUARY 1839 IN THE NINTH YEAR OF HER AGE.

As news spread of the discovery, Dalton family historians began to associate the grave with the 'Sarah Dalton', purported daughter of George III, who married one James Dalton. Again, they asked, why did George III give an expensive organ to an obscure church in Wales? Mystery plied on mystery; was the gift to hallow the place of worship of his daughter? The jury is still out.

Which royal duke married twice – illegally? And which one hated arranged marriages?

Will you allow me to come this evening? It is my only hope. Oh! Let me come, and we will send for Mr Gunn. Everything but this is hateful to me. More than forty-eight hours have passed without the slightest nourishment. Oh, let me not live so … If Gunn will not marry me, I shall die.

HRH Prince Augustus, Duke of Sussex to The Lady Augusta Murray, 4 April 1793.

Prince Augustus Frederick, Duke of Sussex, was born at Buckingham House, St James's Park, 27 January 1773, the sixth son and ninth child of George III and Queen Charlotte. Educated at Göttingen University, along with his brothers Ernest, Duke of Cumberland and Adolphus, Duke of Cambridge, Augustus was not destined for the army like his brothers because of 'convulsive asthma'. He travelled and studied classics at Rome to become something of a scholar; he had a passion for music and books – his 50,000 volume collection included 5,000 bibles. While in Rome he fell into the matrimonial net set out by Lady Charlotte Stewart for her daughter Augusta, the second daughter Lady Charlotte had had by her husband John Murray, 4th Earl of Dunmore. Lady Augusta was five years the prince's senior, was considered 'plain' and had inherited her mother's bossiness.

Following what seems to have been a mutually celibate relationship the prince married Lady Augusta at Rome on 4 April 1793 under the Anglican rite by the Revd Gunn. They were married again at St George's, Hanover Square on 5 December. Both ceremonies were in contravention of the Royal Marriages Act of 1772.

George III was much angered by the illegal marriage and it was declared null and void by the Court of Arches on 3 August 1794. Augustus and Augusta lived together despite all this and two children were born. Sir Augustus Frederick d'Este (1794–1848) was born in Essex and became Deputy Ranger of St James's and Hyde Parks, and unsuccessfully claimed the dukedom of Sussex on his father's death. Augusta Emma d'Este (1801–55) was born at Lower Grosvenor Street, London, and married Thomas Wilde, 1st Baron Truro, who became Lord High Chancellor from 1850–52. Neither of the children left issue.

For years the illegal union alienated Prince Augustus from George III and his Court, but by royal licence in 1806 Lady Augusta assumed the surname of de Ameland and was styled Countess. An estrangement developed between the prince and Augusta and she died at Ramsgate in 1830.

Once again, in contravention of the Royal Marriages Act, around 2 May 1831, Prince Augustus married Lady Cecilia Letitia Underwood, widow of Sir George Buggin and daughter of the 2nd Earl of Arran. Although she was twelve years younger than the prince there were no offspring from the union. Small in stature and quaint in dress, Cecilia was accepted by the Royal Family as the prince's wife, and in 1840 Queen Victoria created her Duchess of Inverness.

While his morganatic illegal wife became a personality in society, Prince Augustus was a great patron of art, science and literature. He was held in great favour by Queen Victoria, who he gave away at her wedding to Prince Albert in 1840. At the time, one wag was heard to remark: 'The Duke of Sussex is always ready to give away what does not belong to him.'

Prince Augustus died of erysipelas at Kensington Palace on 21 April 1843. In his idiosyncratic way he left instructions that he was to be buried at Kensal Green Cemetery, north of Paddington. This is certainly because he wanted, in due time, for his wife to be buried with him; her cadaver would not have been accepted for the royal vault. Lady Cecilia died at Kensington Palace on 1 August 1873.

It was Queen Victoria's wedding day, Monday 10 February 1840. Among the guests that day were the queen's uncles Prince Augustus, Duke of Sussex, who 'sobbed throughout the ceremony' and Prince Adolphus, Duke of Cambridge, who 'made, loud good humoured comments'; alongside them was Cambridge's son Prince George William Frederick Charles, who at 21 was the same age as his cousin the queen. Rumour had it that Prince George had been skulking abroad for some time in case he had been forced to marry Victoria.

He commented to any who cared to hear, 'arranged marriages are doomed to failure'.

George went on to be a field marshal and commander-in-chief of the British Forces from 1856–95, but his marriage caused more scandal in court circles. Later, on the day of Queen Victoria's wedding, Prince George met Sarah – called Louisa – Fairbrother (b.1815), the fifth daughter of Robert and Mary Fairbrother, a theatrical printer family in Covent Garden. Louisa had gone on the stage in 1830 and was a well-known actress in pantomime at the Theatre Royal, Drury Lane, the Lyceum and Covent Garden. Possessed of a captivating charm she was considered a 'classical beauty' and Prince George was instantly smitten. It is likely that Prince George knew that Louisa already had an illegitimate son Charles (1839–1901), whose father was probably Charles John Manners-Sutton, 1st Viscount Canterbury, Speaker of the House of Commons. A relationship developed and marriage was discussed; a marriage that would not have been acceptable to the Royal Family. Nevertheless, and in contravention of the Royal Marriages Act, Prince George and Louisa were married at St John's church, Clerkenwell, on 8 January 1847. Thereafter Louisa was known as 'Mrs FitzGeorge', and took up residence at No. 6 Queen Street, Mayfair, 'where', wrote George's biographer the Revd Edgar Shepperd, 'the Duke devoted to his wife all the hours he could spare from his public duties and private engagements'. Prince George had his official residence at Gloucester House, Piccadilly.

Three children were born of the union. George William Adolphus FitzGeorge (1843–1907), served in the army; Sir Adolphus Augustus FitzGeorge (1846–1922) became a rear admiral, and Sir Augustus Charles Frederick FitzGeorge (1847–1933) also served in the army and was his father's private secretary. Louisa had given birth too, on 22 March 1841, to a daughter Louisa Catherine; she was never openly acknowledged as Prince George's daughter but she took the name FitzGeorge and was frequently at her putative father's house; she died a childless widow in 1919.

Louisa FitzGeorge suffered a distressing two-year illness and died on Sunday 12 January 1870 to be buried in the mausoleum Prince George had erected at Kensal Green. Prince George died at Gloucester House on 17 March 1904. His morganatic illegal marriage was deemed to be a happy one and he openly mourned Louisa's death for the rest of his life. On his wedding day he was to have said this to his new bride:

> You alone know love, or ought to know, how blessed and happy I feel that this day made you my own and me yours.

Who were the youngest royal child grooms and brides to inherit or be consort to the thrones of England and Scotland?

The passion of John for his queen [Isabella of Angoulême], though it was sufficiently strong to embroil him in war, was not exclusively enough to secure conjugal fidelity; the king tormented her with jealousy, while on his part he was far from setting her a good example, for he often invaded the honour of the female nobility.

Agnes Strickland (1796–1874), historian on King John, 1840.

No one had seen the like before as the great English wagon-train trundled through France. Two hundred men-at-arms, knights, clerks, stewards, sergeants, squires and retainers, all led by Thomas Becket, Chancellor of England, slowly made their way through town and village. Crowds flocked to see the five-horse wagons and packhorses loaded with furniture, clothes, food, beer, and chests of gold and silver plate, bound for the French Court. There King Louis VII and his second wife Constance of Castile awaited the marriage proposals carried by Becket from King Henry II of England. In a short time, in that year of 1158, it was agreed that the French king's daughter Marguerite be betrothed to Henry the Younger, eldest surviving son of Henry II and Eleanor of Aquitaine. An early marriage was not contemplated as Marguerite was 2 years old and young Henry 4. They were married though when Henry was crowned King of England in his father's lifetime (a Capetian practice) at Westminster Abbey on 24 May 1170. Henry the Younger never succeeded his father, dying in 1182.

Had Henry the Younger reigned he would have been the youngest monarch to marry, but ten more monarchs and consorts were to marry in the Middle Ages before they were 13. On 24 August 1200, John Lackland, King of England, married Isabella (d.1246), daughter of Count Aymer Taillefer of Angoulême as his second wife. She was just 12 and John just over 32. In his *Chronica Majora* Matthew Paris made this comment on the royal couple:

> He detested his wife and she him. She was an incestuous and depraved woman, so notoriously guilty of adultery that the king had given orders that her lovers were to be seized and throttled on her bed. He himself was envious of many of his barons and kinsfolk, and seduced their more attractive daughters and sisters.

Isabella, it seems, continued to lead a racy life after John's death in 1216.

Henry III (r.1216–72), married off his sister Joan to Alexander II (r.1214–49), King of Scots. At his marriage at York on 18 June 1221, Joan was some ten months over her tenth birthday and Alexander was not yet 23. Joan died in 1238, their marriage being childless; yet this was another political marriage which led to much diplomatic haggling between the two kingdoms. Eleanor, daughter of Count Raymond Berenger of Provence, was around 13 when she married Henry III on 14 January 1236 at Canterbury Cathedral. He was a few months over 28 years old. They were married some thirty-six years, their first child (Edward I) being born in 1239 when Eleanor was 16 and they went on to have eight more children. Another political marriage occurred between Henry III's eldest daughter Margaret (d.1275) and Alexander III (r.1249–86), King of Scots. Margaret was just over 11 years old at the marriage in York on 26 December 1251 and Alexander just over 10; they had three children, all of whom died within five years of their mother.

Historians have described the wedding of 13-year-old Eleanor, daughter of King Ferdinand III of Castile and 15-year-old Edward I (r.1272–1307), at Las Huelgas, Castile, in October 1254, as 'one of the great love matches of history'. They were to have sixteen children. Another long marriage, but childless, was that of David II (r.1329–71), King of Scots, to Joanna (d.1262) daughter of Edward II of England at Berwick-upon Tweed on 17 July 1328. David – the heir to King Robert I, the Bruce – was just over 4 years old and Joanna 7. Another heir to the throne, like David II, was Henry Boilinbroke, when he married Mary (d.1394) daughter of Humphrey de Bohun, Earl of Warwick, at Arundel, Sussex on 3 April 1367. She was around 11 years of age and Henry just over 13. Mary gave birth at 13 and Henry ruled as Henry IV (r.1399–1413). One marriage never consummated was that of Richard II (r.1377–99) to Isabella (d.1409), daughter of Charles VI of France. Richard was then 29 and Isaballa 6 years old. The marriage was part of a peace treaty between England and France.

Scotland's kingdom was expanded when James III (r.1460–88) married Margaret (d.1486), daughter of Christian I of Denmark, at Holyrood Abbey on 10 July 1469, for her dowry included the islands of Orkney and Shetland. The last of the young marriages of the Middle Ages was that of Margaret Tudor, daughter of Henry VII to James IV (r.1488–1513), King of Scots at Holyrood Abbey on 8 August 1503. Margaret was around 13 and James 30 years old. Through this marriage, 100 years later, the thrones of England and Scotland were united under James I/VI.

Did British monarchs use contraceptives?

A Gentleman of this House [Wills Coffee House, 1 Bow Street, London] ... observ'd by the Surgeons with much Envy; for he has invented an Engine for the Prevention of Harms by Love-Adventures and has, by great Care and Application made it an Immodesty to name his Name.

'On the inventor of the condom', Tatler Magazine, *1709*.

In the picture archives of the British Library there is a print of 1744 dubbed 'Quality control in a condom warehouse'. It shows a gentleman purchaser offering his fee while a seated woman blows into the contraceptive he is about to buy to test its capability. On a table lies a range of condoms of different sizes in production while a clergyman blesses the merchandise. On the floor a cat and dog fight over a discarded condom; above them a line of condoms are suspended of prodigious sizes. The business looks prosperous, but Britain always lagged behind other nations when it came to contraception. Condoms were known among those who felt need of them from the seventeenth century. The first recorded modern mention of them is in Gabriello Falloppio's *De Morbo Gallico* published after the author's death in 1564. Even so there was a persistent belief throughout the eighteenth century that condoms were a British invention.

Better-off men in the eighteenth century probably used condoms to protect themselves from venereal diseases when consorting with street whores. From the early 1700s condoms were available from London street sellers in St James's Park, Spring Gardens, the Play-House and the Mall. Mostly made of animal membrane, biographer James Boswell noted in his *London Journal* for Saturday 4 June 1763, that the condoms worked best if they were first dipped in the lake at St James's Park. Soldiers used them even earlier; such a condom dating from around 1650 was found in a cesspit at Dudley Castle.

There were a range of 'contraceptive potions' available from apothecaries, but they were disdained by many, as were other contraceptive techniques such as the rhythm method, *coitus interruptus* and saline douches. It was not until 1823 that contraception was given a public airing by political radical Francis Place in his handbill *To the Married of Both Sexes.* Ideas on contraception were also taken up by a printer called Richard Carlile in his journal *The Republican*, and later in 1825 in a full publication *Every Woman's Book; or, What is Love?* A boost to such publications was given by philosopher John Stuart Mill who circulated them while a junior clerk in the India Office. Socialist Robert Dale Owen in his *Moral Physiology* (1830) advocated the 'complete withdrawal method' while George Drysdale's *Elements of Social Science* (1854) offered 'five techniques of contraception'.

The high incidence of illegitimacy among British royal houses from the days of Henry I (d.1131), with his estimated twenty-five illegitimate children at least, would suggest that contraception was not high on the list of royal concerns. One popular story has it that a 'royal physician', one 'Dr Condom', invented the preventative sheath to help Charles II reduce the roll of his illegitimate children; there seems to have been a decided lack of success as the king had at least sixteen illegitimates by some eight mistresses. A pamphlet issued around 1690 entitled *Duchess of Portsmouth's Garland* has Charles II's mistress Louise Renee de Kéroüalle (Duchess of Portsmouth) using 'new fashioned sponges to clear her … from slimy sperm'. Dr Condom – whoever he was – did not invent the sheath. The Ancient Egyptians beat him to it as a sketch of the XIX Dynasty (1350–1200 BC) shows.

Other monarchs had more diverse difficulties than Charles II. His brother James II/VII and his wife Mary of Modena took the waters of Bath to produce a male heir, and it is thought that Queen Anne visited the town for the same purpose.

By the reign of Queen Victoria, from 1837, 'a pall of prudery lay over nineteenth century England'; methods of contraception were little known, or spoken about, and were considered 'not respectable'. Although printed adverts for condoms did not appear until the early years of Edward VII's reign – whether he availed himself of them during his career of serial adultery is not known – their mention in the press always caused a public sensation. For eighteen days during November–December 1886, the nation was spellbound by the Campbell *versus* Campbell legal case. This evolved after the collapse of the marriage of Lord Colin Campbell – fifth son of George, 8th Duke of Argyll – and his wife, the former Gertrude Blood. Lord Colin accused his wife of adultery with Charles Spencer Churchill, Duke of Marlborough, General William Butler and London's fire chief Captain Eyre Massey Shaw, and others. Lady Campbell counterclaimed.

Calling before Sir Charles Parker Butt, the trial included an examination of the Campbells's sex life. Answering a question from lawyer Frank Lockwood, Lady Campbell admitted that contraceptives had been used during their sexual intercourse. This was because Lord Colin was thought to have syphilis. This gave rise to the public belief that contraception was in regular use among the upper classes in their adulterous relationships. Both the Campbells were exonerated at the trial. Lord Colin died in 1895 and Lady Campbell in 1911. Although her life had more to it than the promiscuity of earlier years – which earned her the title of Victorian 'Sex Goddess' – her court appearance added a facet or two to the history of Victorian contraception. With her brood of nine children Queen Victoria and Prince Albert seem not to have practiced contraception. Even so, Frenchman Hector France found in London's Petticoat Lane, a vendor selling condoms bearing the portrait of Queen Victoria.

Whatever advice on contraception was given to royalty by their physicians, one royal doctor's opinion was clear. While the Lambeth Conference of Bishops of 1920 condemned the use of 'artificial means of restriction', physician-extraordinary to George V, Lord Dawson of Penn, denounced the conference's opinions in these terms:

> The love envisaged by the Lambeth Conference is an invertebrate, joyless thing – not worth having. Birth control is here to stay.

The royal doctor made the headlines with his opinion of contraception, a feat not repeated since the days of Charles II.

Murders, Plots
and Assassinations

Who shot King Harold in the eye?

... a shower of arrows fell round King Harold, and he himself was
pierced in the eye. A crowd of horsemen now burst in, and the
King, already wounded, was slain.

Archdeacon Henry of Huntingdon in Historia Anglorum *(1154).*

Look along the length of the Bayeux Tapestry and pause at
section 29 and there you'll find him. *Hic dederunt Haroldo
corona Regis* (Here they give Harold the king's crown), reads
the heading caption, describing how the Witangemot (assembly of
nobles) offers to Harold Godwineson the diadem that makes him
Harold II, King of the English. Harold (b. *c.* 1022) was crowned on
6 January 1066 at Westminster Abbey, in the full knowledge that on
the death of his brother-in-law Edward the Confessor (d. 4 January
1066), said French sources, William, Duke of Normandy would be

recognised as heir instead of Edward's grandson Edgar the Aetheling. Harold had already paid homage to William in this connection. So Harold's action precipitated the most famous battle on English soil at Senlac Hill, north of Hastings, on 14 October 1066.

The 70m long Bayeux Tapestry, often known as 'Queen Matilda's Tapestry', is purported to have been commissioned some ten years after the battle by William the Conqueror's half-brother Odo de Conteville, Bishop of Bayeux. Its embroidery, tradition tells us, was carried out by Matilda, Queen of England, Duchess of Normandy, and her ladies; its length depicting her husband William's exploits and the events of the battle.

On 25 September 1066 at Stamford Bridge, Harold defeated the combined forces of his traitorous exiled brother Tostig, Earl of Northumberland and Harald Hardrada of Norway, bent on seizing the realm. By this time William and his Norman army had landed at Pevensey and Harold prepared to confront the invaders. The details of the Battle of Hastings are well known; William won the day and the kingdom, but Harold's death is still a matter of historical contention. Section 57 of the Bayeux Tapestry bears the caption: *Hic Harold Rex interfectus est* (Here King Harold dies). The panel shows a knight pulling an arrow out of his head; next to him is a mounted soldier hacking at a falling knight. But which figure is Harold? Are they both Harold? Certainly the first figure gives rise to the famous story of Harold being killed by an arrow in the eye. If it is accepted that the Bayeux Tapestry is a piece of Norman propaganda to boost William's exploits, as the tapestry says (panel 58) *Hic Franci pugnant et ceciderunt quierant cum Haraldo* (Here the French fight and Harold's followers succumb), the arrow in the eye might be a medieval metaphor for a punishment for Harold for reneging on his oath to William. So the second figure may be Harold too being finally slain by the mounted knight. This would back up what Henry of Huntingdon wrote. Interestingly, Professor David Bernstein in Morillo's *The Battle of Hastings* notes that he saw a line of small holes in the fabric 'leading to the fallen figure's forehead ...' Was there once another arrow here, removed by the embroiderers? Berstein thinks that this is proof of Harold's infamy being underlined, as blindness was the medieval metaphor for divine punishment.

Was King William II, 'Rufus' murdered?

Here stood the oak tree in which an arrow shot by Sir Walter Tyrell [*sic*] at a stag glanced and struck King William the Second, surnamed Rufus, on the breast of which he died instantly on the second day of August anno 1100.

Rufus Stone set up in the New Forest by Lord John Delaware, 1745.

William II, by-named 'Rufus' because of his ruddy cheeks and red hair, son of William the Conqueror and his wife Queen Matilda of Flanders, was born in Normandy around 1057. Although his father's favourite son, William had a bad press mostly because of his heavy hand with the Church. Here's what the *Anglo-Saxon Chronicle* says about him after his death:

In his days, therefore righteousness declined and evil of every kind towards God and man put up its head. He oppressed the Church of God ... I may be delaying too long over all these matters, but everything that was hateful to God and to righteous men was the daily practice in this land during his reign. Therefore he was hated by almost all his people and abhorrent to God. This his end testified, for he died in the midst of his sins without repentence or any atonement for his evil deeds.

Today it is difficult to obtain an objective assessment of William Rufus. Contemporary chronicles – written by monks – were prejudiced against him. They pointed out that he was opinionated, arrogant, irascible, irreligious, and avaricious. This was the opinion, too, of historians into the nineteenth century, but more recent scholars have moderated the view of William Rufus. It is true that he had powerful enemies among his barons, family conflicts added to opposition and there were those who, because he never married, smeared him further as a homosexual. William of Malmesbury stated that William's court was effeminate with young men who 'rival women in delicacy of person, to mince their gait, to walk with loose gestures and half naked'. Nevertheless William seems to have been a competent soldier and was an able and capable king, who achieved working relationships with Malcolm III of Scots and the Welsh princes. Yet his temperament and pretensions annoyed both prelate and noble. All of this led to the speculation as to the manner of William Rufus's death.

On the first evening of August 1100 William Rufus and a party of seven, including his brother Count Henry Beauclerc, William de Breteuil, Robert FitzHamon and Walter Tirel, Lord of Poix in Normandy, slept at a hunting lodge near Brokenhurst in the New Forest. The next afternoon they set off for the chase. Assisted by huntsmen the party took up their positions in groups. William Rufus and Tirel placed themselves, waiting for the huntsmen to drive the game towards them. A deer broke cover as the sun was sinking, and William Rufus fired an arrow which wounded the beast, but not fatally. As William Rufus watched the deer's movements and the sun dazzled over the forest, another deer came into view and this time Tirel loosed an arrow, but hit the king instead. Breaking off the arrow William Rufus fell from his horse, falling onto the broken arrow shaft which penetrated deeper and hastened his end. Tirel dismounted, examined the unconscious king and then, to future historians' puzzlement, leapt on his horse and galloped away. The contemporary accounts of what actually happened are confusing. Immediately it was proclaimed an accident, with Tirel identified as the unfortunate perpetrator. But was William Rufus deliberately slain?

Historians have gathered to present theory after conspiracy theory concerning William Rufus's death. For instance, Duncan Grinnell-Milne, in his *The Killing of William Rufus* believes that the death was part of a plan by William Rufus's brother, Count Henry Beauclerc, to attain the throne; he was crowned King of England at Westminster on 6 August 1100. If this were so, Henry had to move fast. William Rufus's chosen heir, his brother Robert, Duke of Normandy, was due back from crusade with a wife and legitimate son. So Henry had a motive for murder to clear the throne before Robert's return. In the king's hunting party were men loyal to Henry and a hunt was a good opportunity to make murder look like an accident. Henry was a ruthless character who was, as biographer James Chambers commented, 'at least capable of contemplating [murder]'. On the evening of that fateful day, Henry left the New Forest at a gallop to secure the royal treasury.

It is interesting to note that Tirel was married to Alice de Clare, whose brothers Gilbert de Clare, Earl of Tunbridge, and Roger de Clare, were Henry's men and were present in the hunting party that day. It is thought that Tirel's rapid flight from the scene was assisted by the de Clares; Tirel did not know the terrain for a rapid escape and a ship was conveniently waiting to take him to France. It cannot be proved that Henry played an active part in his brother's death, although he had a strong motive to be so involved. As Emma Mason has pointed out in her biography of William Rufus, Henry 'seemed well prepared for the eventuality [of his brother's death] and assured of powerful backers in his bid for the throne'. Certainly the de Clares did well out of Henry's rise, with gifts of land and prominent positions in church preferment and at court. Did Tirel sacrifice himself for the de Clares advantage? He lived in exile but his lands in England and France were never confiscated as one would have expected had he been deemed guilty of murder.

The official verdict of accidental death was never officially challenged, although Tirel did always swear that he was innocent of murder. There was no official investigation. William Rufus's body was hastily conveyed onto a charcoal-burner's cart from the New Forest to Winchester for burial. His bones were not to be given eternal rest. In 1107 the great tower of Winchester Cathedral collapsed. William of Malmesbury noted that people gossiped that the tower's collapse, smashing William Rufus's tomb, was 'divine disapproval' of his character. William Rufus was reburied at more than one site in the cathedral until his bones were placed in a tomb chest above the screen on the north side of the presbytery. During the English Civil War these mortuary chests were hauled down by Cromwell's troops and the bones of William Rufus, King Cnut, Queen Emma and their son King Harthacnut (and others) were used as missiles to smash the cathedral windows. Later the bones were collected up and mixed up in the mortuary chests where they remain today.

Is it true that Henry II was responsible for Thomas Becket's death?

What miserable drones and traitors have I nourished and promoted in my household, who let their lord be treated with such shameful contempt by a low-born clerk.

> *Henry II expressing his anger at Thomas Becket as quoted by*
> *the archbishop's biographer and witness of his murder*
> *Edward Grim (fl. 1170–77).*

On 29 December 1170, Thomas Becket, Archbishop of Canterbury, was murdered in his cathedral of Christ Church, Canterbury.

The perpetrators were four Norman knights – close associates of King Henry II – Reginald FitzUrse, Hugh de Morville, William de Tracy and Richard le Breton.

The story of Thomas Becket's martyrdom is perhaps the most famous ecclesiastical murder of all time, the power of his personality transcending almost nine centuries. He has been the subject of countless biographies and internationally acclaimed plays by such as T.S. Eliot (*Murder in the Cathedral*, 1935) and Jean Anouilh (*Becket*, 1961). Born around 1118, the son of a Norman merchant, he was educated by the Augustinians at Merton Priory, London and Paris to become a notary and entered the service of Archbishop Theobald of Canterbury. Against a background of royal turmoil when various contenders were claiming the English throne, Thomas studied canon law at Auxerre and Bologna. In the year Henry Curtmantle was crowned Henry II, Thomas was appointed to the important archdeaconship of Canterbury in the Church that was still the repository of most of the learning and much of the law that applied to Christendom in general and England in particular.

Thomas Becket's talents were impressive and in 1155 Henry II made him Chancellor of England, a role Thomas threw himself into with great vigour and enthusiasm. An extraordinary intimacy sprang up between them and Thomas pursued Henry's policies with relish. Thomas even devised taxes (which fell heavily on the Church) to pay for Henry's expedition against Toulouse in 1159. In 1161 Archbishop Theobald died and Henry saw a wonderful opportunity to subjugate the Church to the State. He would make his own man Thomas Becket Archbishop of Canterbury. It took Thomas a year to accept; in 1162 he became archbishop but refused to remain Chancellor. On the appointment a change came over him, and herein for historians lies the enigma of Thomas Becket.

Despite the fact that he engendered a tax that had been hard on the Church in 1159 – as one chronicler put it, 'Having in his hand the sword of state, he plunged it into the bosom of the church, his mother' – as archbishop did he now feel he owed a greater loyalty to the church 'his mother' rather than the king? Or did he see himself now as more powerful than when he was Chancellor? Whatever Thomas now believed his quarrels with the king became stormy and regular. In 1163 he successfully defied the king on a point of taxation at the council at Woodstock; the first time this had ever happened in English history. Their quarrels reverberated across Europe. Thomas endeavoured to reclaim Church property from the Crown; he prohibited the marriage of Henry II's brother William of Anjou to the Countess de Warenne; he opposed royal jurisdiction over 'criminous clerks in holy orders' and these activities went on and on until Thomas was forced to flee to France. Even in exile he called the king's authority into question. Thus, he became a thorn in Henry II's side.

Thomas remained in exile for six years but returned on 1 December 1170 following a reconciliation with Henry, however, he had no intention of knuckling down to the royal will or to the English bishops whom he had also thwarted and excommunicated. Henry flew into one of his rages when in France he heard of Thomas's latest rulings. Henry's fury ended with the frenzied question: Was there no one in his entourage who would protect him from this low-born priest? Four of his knights slipped away and crossed the Channel in great secrecy. The rapidity of their departure begs the question: Were they anxious to act before Henry withdrew his words? After all, it had happened many times before; Henry was free with his statements often regretting them afterwards. But even so, his words on Thomas could not normally be interpreted as a licence to murder.

So that is how Thomas Becket came to be murdered and strangely the outcome was a victory for both Thomas and Henry. On 21 February 1173 Pope Alexander III canonised Thomas, and he entered history as a Christian martyr. His shrine remained a focus for pilgrims until in 1538 Henry VIII declared that Thomas was murdered as a defender of 'his usurped authority, and a bearer of the iniquity of the clergy'. In death Thomas had secured the Church's independence from the Crown under the law which remained until the Reformation.

As for Henry II he was rid of the most serious challenge to his kingship, although overall he had set in motion a political blunder. His rash words had been a catalyst for Thomas's murder and, apart from being under ecclesiastical censure, none in England pointed a finger at Henry as having ordered Thomas Becket's death. Even John of Salisbury, later Bishop of Chartres, who was with Thomas at the time of the murder, makes no mention of the king's possible culpability in his chronicles. Yet, William of Sens, also later Bishop of Chartres, said that 'the King admitted … that he had provided the cause of Thomas's death and had in effect killed him'. Somewhat tardy in his efforts at exoneration, eventually in 1174 Henry did public penance at Thomas's tomb in Canterbury Cathedral, where he was scourged at the hands of the monks of Christ Church.

Did Queen Isabella order the death of Edward II?

She-wolf of France, with unrelenting fangs,
That tear'st the bowels of thy mangled mate.
'The Bard' (1757) by Thomas Gray (1716–71).

Set out on the chessboard the queen is a formidable piece; no more trenchant Queen of England ever played in the game of medieval chess between England and France than the beautiful 'she-wolf' Isabella, daughter of the Capetian Philip IV – Philippe Le Bel – of France and his wife Johanna I of Navarre. On 25 January 1308 at the cathedral church of Notre Dame at Boulogne, the 12-year-old Isabella married by papal dispensation Edward II (b.1284), King of England for six months since the death of his father Edward I, 'Longshanks'. As Elizabeth Longford noted, she 'is probably the most vilified of England's queens'.

Edward II's reign has received scathing analysis, for instance, T.F. Tout in *Edward I* (1890) identified him as 'a coward and a trifler'. Edward spent the bulk of his reign opposing his barons not on great issues, but to defend his favourites: the Gascon Piers Gaveston, with whom he had fallen in love as a teenager, and Hugh le Despencer.

Although Edward seemed captivated by his new wife, from her landing at Dover on 2 February 1308, Isabella realised that Piers Gaveston, now Earl of Cornwall, would appear the greater in Edward's affections than she did. At Edward's coronation on 25 February, Gaveston not Isabella was guest of honour. It was a grave insult to France and on that day Edward sowed the seeds of his ultimate fate.

From the first too, Edward was mean to Isabella: she was given no dower lands, patronage nor finances to run her household. As a consequence Isabella's father encouraged England's rebel barons to rise up against Edward. The king now tried to mollify France; Isabella was granted title to the English estates in France, and she was given greater honour at court. Nevertheless, her hatred of Gaveston, now exiled with honour as Regent in Ireland, simmered intensely.

Slowly Isabella's influence and wealth increased as Edward loosened the purse strings. All the while Edward was threatened by his barons, and on the borders with Scotland, King Robert I, the Bruce, loomed hostile with guerrilla raids. On 19 May 1312 the barons caught up with the hated Gaveston, long returned from Ireland, and he was executed as a traitor. Edward was devastated. More seriously the country teetered on civil war.

The birth of Isabella's first child in 1312 proved to be another friction with France; Edward had to concede to the barons that the child should not be called Louis (after Isabella's great-grandfather), and thus was born the future Edward III. Crises continued in Scotland. By 1313 the English overlordship hammered home by Edward I was reduced to one castle, Stirling, now under siege by King Robert's brother. Edward was forced to send troops to support Stirling's governor Sir Philip de Mowbray. Outnumbered two to one the Scots still trounced the English at the Battle of Bannockburn on 24 June 1314 and Edward's reputation was at its nadir.

For the next ten years Edward struggled with opposing factions in his realm which descended into anarchy. He listened only to his court favourites (the Despencers), an attachment that caused Isabella's ultimate alienation from Edward. A truce was finally agreed with Scotland in 1323, but in Wales the most powerful marcher, Lord Roger Mortimer, saw the Despencers as meddlers in his domain. Urged on by the Despencers, Edward rode against Mortimer who was captured and imprisoned in the Tower. Although she bore Edward four children, Edward, John of Eltham, Eleanor and Joan, Isabella became more and more distant from Edward. In fact, Geoffrey le Baker (fl.1350) in his *Chronicle* (*c*.1341) noted that Isabella worked out 'the perfect murder' in collusion with Mortimer and the Bishop of Hereford. Isabella had now formed a close acquaintanceship with Mortimer which led to her falling in love with him. As the Tower was also a palace as well as a prison Isabella had early contact with Mortimer. Again relations with France deteriorated and Isabella suggested that she try to negotiate with her brother Charles IV. She went to France and there she was joined by Mortimer whose escape from the Tower she had engineered. They now dwelt openly in France as lovers. Thus wrote Elizabeth Longford, 'she was the only medieval queen known to have been an adulteress'.

Isabella and Mortimer raised an army to depose Edward and replace him with her son; she now led the revolution that sealed her husband's fate. Her army landed at Harwich in September

1326 and eventually Edward was captured in Wales and taken to Kenilworth Castle.

On 25 January 1327 Edward II abdicated in favour of his son and was taken to Berkley Castle, Gloucestershire. An attempt to rescue him failed. He must not be allowed to escape and make a resurgence, said his enemies, so Roger Mortimer made arrangements for his death. It is too incredible to believe that Isabella did not know the murder plans. Historians believe that both Isabella and Edward expected the other to seek their murder. Edward cannot be said to have been a loving husband. In the Chartulary of Winchester Cathedral is this comment (1334) by the then Bishop of Winchester: 'The king carried a knife in his hose to kill queen Isabella, and [Edward] said that if he had no other weapon he would crush her with his teeth.'

The death of Edward would have to appear natural. Starvation did not work, neither did exposing him to the rotting carcasses of his dead subjects, so said Augustinian friar John Capgrave (1393–1464) in his *Chronicle*:

> Edward [was] slain with a hot spit put into his body [i.e. his anus] which could not be spied when he was dead for they put a horn into his tewhel [rectum] and the spit through the horn that there should be no burning appear outside. This was by the ordinance as was said of Sir John Maltravers [Edward's jailer] and Thomas Gournay, which laid a great door upon him while they did their work.

Edward II was buried at Gloucester Cathedral. Edward's death was not avenged until 1330. Roger Mortimer was tried and executed at Tyburn; Isabella was confined under house arrest at Castle Rising, Norfolk. Some chroniclers say that she became unhinged at Mortimer's execution. She died on 22 August 1358 and was buried at Greyfriar's church, Newgate, London. Hypocritically, historians note she was buried with Edward's heart on her chest.

Could Richard III be innocent of the death of the 'Princes in the Tower'?

... But after Easter [1484] much whispering was among the people that the king [Richard III] had put the children of King Edward to death.

The Great Chronicle of London *(1504)*.

In 1951 the Scottish novelist and playwright Josephine Tey (Elizabeth Mackintosh, 1897–1955) produced her book *The Daughter of Time* in which she explored the historical murder story of the 'Princes in the Tower'. She opens the story by having her lead character Inspector Grant stuck in hospital and bored. He is brought a selection of photographs to entertain him, one of which is of King Richard III taken from his portrait in the National Gallery. At first Grant assumes that the portrait is of a judge, or at least someone in great authority. He is staggered to learn that it is of the 'hunchback who murdered his nephews' as depicted by William Shakespeare. Spurred on he re-examines the evidence and decides Richard was vilified in a Tudor plot. Josephine Tey brought the puzzle once more into the public domain; but was her conclusion of Richard III's innocence of murder plausible?

On May Day 1464 at Grafton Regis, Northampton, Edward IV of the House of York, then 22, married in secret the widow of Sir John Gray called Elizabeth Woodville, daughter of the 1st Lord Rivers; she already had two children. Once the marriage was announced there was consternation. It was rumoured that Edward was already married to Lady Eleanor Butler, daughter of the Earl of Shrewsbury.

By Elizabeth, Edward had ten children, of whom many considered all to be illegitimate. Edward IV died at the Palace of Westminster, 9 April 1483, to be succeeded by his son and fourth child as Edward V, aged 13. He and his brother Richard, Duke of York, became the famous 'Princes in the Tower'. Young Edward grew up in a court circle riven with hostility between Edward IV and his brothers, George, Duke of Clarence (executed in 1478, traditionally drowned in a butt of malmsey wine) and Richard, Duke of Gloucester. On Edward IV's death Gloucester engineered events to become Lord High Protector, a step in his plan to take the throne. He managed to install the youngsters Edward and Richard in the Tower, at that time still a royal residence. Gloucester then took steps to have his nephews accepted as illegitimate, and Edward was deposed as king on 25 June 1483. Gloucester assumed the throne the next day as Richard III. After this, the young boys seem to have vanished from public sight. Down the centuries what happened to them is a matter of conjecture.

A study of contemporary 'evidence', like that found in the *Croyland Chronicle*, supplies only gossip, hearsay and rumour. An Italian clerk called Dominic Mancini wrote in 1483 an account of his stay in England. He left one of the few contemporary comments about what people were saying about the princes' fate:

> He [Edward V] ... and his brother were withdrawn into the inner apartments of the Tower proper, and day by day began to be seen more rarely behind the bars and windows, till at length they ceased to appear altogether. A Strasbourg doctor, the last of his attendants whose services the King enjoyed, reported that the young King, like a victim prepared for sacrifice, sought remission of his sins by daily confession and penance, because he believed that death was facing him.

Mancini also repeated the rumour:

> ... that the sons of King Edward had died a violent death, but it was uncertain how.

Documentation only shows one 'outright accusation of murder'. It records a speech made before the Estates General by the French Chancellor de Rochford, dated January 1484. The Chancellor asks delegates to remember and pray for the two children of Edward IV 'whose massacre went unpunished, while the assassin was crowned by popular assent'.

Had the two boys died of natural causes? If so, why did Richard not make this known? Others believe that the boys lived on to be murdered on the orders of Richard III's successor, Henry VII, after the Battle of Bosworth Field. The whole fate of the boys remained so secret that the pretenders Lambert Simnel and Perkin Warbeck were able to achieve some credibility as the lost boys.

In 1647 the remains of two young children were found buried in an elm chest on a staircase in the Tower. From the location of the box in the White Tower and the approximate ages of the skeletons they were treated as the bones of the two princes and reburied in Westminster Abbey. The burial urn's Latin epitaph boldly states that Richard III had them 'smothered … with pillows'. In 1933 the bones were subjected to forensic examination by anatomist Professor William Wright and Lawrence Tanner. From their study of the bone formation and the development of the teeth it was suggested that the skeletons were of boys aged about 12 and 10. Such ages would tally with the ages of the two princes at the time of their disappearance in 1483. Further research on the skeletons in the early 1960s seemed to confirm the original assessment. The identity of the bones remains inconclusive. Thus the supposed murder of the princes has long been laid at the door of Richard III, but all the evidence is circumstantial, the historical waters muddied by Tudor propagandists Polydore Vergil in *Anglicae Historiae* and Sir Thomas More's *History of Richard III*. Although written in 1513, some thirty years after the events, More's account of the supposed murders by Richard III had a great influence on what people thought about the princes' deaths, and more boldly, declared Richard as ordering their murder:

And forasmuch as [Richard's] mind gave him that, his nephews living, men would not reckon that he could have right to the realm, he thought therefore without delay to rid them, as though the killing of his kinsmen could amend his cause and make him kindly King. Whereupon he sent one John Green, whom he specially trusted, unto Sir Robert Brackenbury, constable of the Tower, with a letter and credence also that the same Sir Robert should in any wise put the two children to death.

Brackenbury refused to carry out the killing, but Richard, said More, selected Sir James Tyrell, Master of the Horse, to carry out his orders. Tyrell recruited a known murderer Miles Forest and stableman John Dighton to murder the boys. More averred that Sir James had confessed his complicity in the murder; he was executed for treason in 1502. The supposed confession of Tyrell lacks credibility. Every so often a book appears in an endeavour to exonerate Richard III, and his innocence is regularly attested by such as the Richard III Society. Nevertheless, taken even at its lowest value, the circumstantial evidence does show that Richard III committed regicide of one boy and murder of the other.

What made Queen Mary I 'Bloody'?

Popular opinion inclines to the view that [Queen Mary's subtitle of Bloody] is attributable to her partiality for the executions of persons she disliked, and particularly to her passionate desire to exterminate the leaders of the Protestant Church ...

Lord Chief Justice Patrick Hastings (1880–1952),
Famous and Infamous Cases *(1950).*

Born at Greenwich Palace, London, on 18 February 1516, Mary Tudor was the only surviving daughter of Henry VIII by his wife Catherine of Aragon. She was crowned at Westminster Abbey by Stephen Gardiner, Bishop of Winchester, on 1 October 1553, three months after her accession.

Mary had a troubled childhood. At first she was adored and cherished by her parents, then, as a consequence of her father's divorce from Catherine of Aragon, her loving father turned into a distant, frightening tyrant, intolerant of her defence of her mother. Mary pursued a rumbustious and violent relationship with her new stepmother Anne Boleyn. In 1533 Mary was declared a bastard, unfit to inherit her father's throne, and was made to wait on her baby half-sister Elizabeth, whom Anne Boleyn had given birth to at Greenwich on 7 September. Mary was treated with humiliating cruelty, with Anne Boleyn often urging King Henry to have Mary put to death. Mary never acknowledged Anne Boleyn as queen.

In 1536 Catherine of Aragon died of cancer and Anne Boleyn was executed for adultery and plotting regicide, but Henry's new wife Jane Seymour begged that Mary be allowed to return to court. Henry would only agree if Mary attested to a document that declared that her mother's marriage was incestuous and unlawful. Mary baulked, but pressured by her father and her cousin Charles V, the Holy Roman Emperor, she signed the document. She never forgave herself for betraying her mother, which was another poisonous stress in her mind. Mary remained in court circles through her father and brother's reigns, to become, as the Imperial ambassador Eustache Chapuys said, 'universally adored' by the king's subjects.

Mary was well-educated, a keen musician and was deemed a possessor of courage, steadfastness and compassion. Yet she was rigid in her devotion to her Roman Catholic faith which would, in the end, warp her underlying natural kind and affectionate nature. Her declared illegitimacy made it difficult to marry her off to various

European princes; she entered spinsterhood, she said, as 'the most unhappy lady in Christendom'. She retreated more into her faith. She despised the Reformed faith gaining strength in England and considered the Protestant faith a threat to 'the traditional concept of an ordered world'. Such a threat she believed must be countered in every possible way; she believed that God wanted all of the 'true faith' to ruthlessly stamp out Protestant 'heresies'.

Mary had red hair, a pale complexion and was of small stature, but her thin lips and piercing stare (caused by poor eyesight) often gave her a sinister expression. As she grew into adulthood she was beset by illness and a longing for marriage and children led her to bouts of frustration. At length she did marry, but her union in July 1554 to the widowed Roman Catholic Philip of Spain, was extremely unpopular in England. Politico-religious opposition to her grew manifest in the insurrection of Sir Thomas Wyatt and Sir James Crofts; the intended coup was badly planned and many of the ringleaders were executed. The failure of the insurrection was a turning point in Mary's reign and marked the beginning of Mary's 'reign of terror' for Protestants and religious Dissenters that would earn her the reputation of 'bloody'.

In 1554 the papal legate Cardinal Reginald Pole (whose attainder under Henry VIII was reversed by Mary), announced England's reconciliation with Rome. Protestantism would be crushed and a papal requirement stated that all heretics be burned at the stake. The re-enactment of the *Statute De Heretico Comburendo* led to the burning of bishops like Hugh Latimer of Worcester and Nicholas Ridley of London. The series of pitiful recantations and the courageous death in March 1556 of the aged, frail Thomas Cranmer, Archbishop of Canterbury was a step too far. It is said: 'Cranmer's martyrdom was the death-blow of Catholicism in England.' The dioceses of Canterbury and London saw the most victims of Mary's fanaticism wherein about 300 suffered horrific martyrdom. Generations thereafter learned of Mary's bloody deeds and the sombre tales of Protestant martyrdom from John Foxe's (d.1587) *The Book of Martyrs*. For centuries its volume of gruesome illustrations of hangings, burnings and garottings took its place alongside the Bible as the two books even the uneducated knew. The book has been decried as 'that huge dunghill of your stinking martyrs, full of a thousand lies'. Nevertheless, it is the only record of the horrors of Marian fanaticism and an important volume in the history of perverted religious dogma.

Ultimately the Marian persecutions failed, and Mary's last years were miserable. Although in love with her husband, he found her repellent, largely because of her syphilitic rhinitis. He went back to Spain in 1557 never to return. A phantom pregnancy led Mary to depression and her belief that her reign was a total failure was underlined in 1558 when the Duke of Guise captured Calais, England's last possession in France. Mary's dream of a Roman Catholic Europe with England as a jewel alongside the Catholic Empire of the Habsburgs came to nothing. Mary died at St James's Palace, 17 November 1558 as a consequence of influenza, to be buried in a tomb in the north aisle of Henry VII's Chapel, Westminster Abbey.

Revisionist historians have endeavoured to show that Mary was 'not by nature a cruel or vindictive woman'. The fires of Smithfield, however, were a consequence of her religious bigotry and have assured that the name 'Bloody Mary' has stuck down the centuries.

How many plots were there to kill Elizabeth I?

There are more than two hundred men of all ages who, at the instigation of the Jesuits, conspire to kill me.

Queen Elizabeth I to the French ambassador,
December 1583.

During her reign of forty-five years Queen Elizabeth I had a number of personal 'alarums'. In October 1583 the clearly insane Roman Catholic John Somerville from Warwickshire, stirred up by anti-Elizabeth Jesuit propaganda, set out with a pistol to assassinate the queen; he hoped, he said, 'to see her head on a pole, for she was a serpent and a viper'. Somerville was arrested, found guilty and condemned to death. Before the hangman could carry out the sentence, Somerville hanged himself in his cell at the Tower of London.

In 1584 a Welsh MP, Dr William Parry, secreted himself in the queen's garden at Richmond Palace, intent on murdering her. On her arrival with her ladies, Parry was 'so daunted with the majesty of her presence in which he saw the image of her father, King Henry VIII' he could not carry out the deed. The reason for Parry's assassination attempt is obscure. He was known to be a spy for William Cecil, Lord Burley, and purported to act as a regicide 'in order to infiltrate papist circles'. This was enough to win him a pension from the queen. Yet there were others who believed he acted with papal blessing on behalf of Mary, Queen of Scots and Parry did boast that he would assassinate the queen if the occasion arose. Whatever the truth was, Parry paid the price for his activities and loose tongue on the gallows.

Again, one day when Queen Elizabeth's barge was plying the Thames, a shot was fired from the shore. One of her bargemen was wounded and the queen handed him her handkerchief to staunch the blood. 'Be of good cheer,' she told him, 'for you will never want. For the bullet was meant for me.'

Plots and intrigues against Elizabeth were everyday fodder for the Elizabethan secret service in London, headed by Sir Francis Walsingham (c.1530–90) who rose to be Secretary of State. Three plots stand out as the most dangerous to Elizabeth. All were Roman Catholic inspired, for in 1570 Pope Pius V issued the *Bull Regnans in Excelsis of Excommunication and Deposition* against Elizabeth, thus giving Catholics a free hand to oppose her. In 1571 strong penal statutes were passed against Roman Catholics.

1571: *The Ridolfi Plot*

Intention: To assassinate Elizabeth. To marry Mary, Queen of Scots to Thomas Howard, 4th Duke of Norfolk (1536–72) and thereafter Catholic soldiers would invade England and put Mary, Queen of Scots on the English throne with Norfolk. Philip of Spain and the Pope backed the move in principle.

The plot was named after a Florentine banker and papal agent called Roberto Ridolfi who acted as go-between for Norfolk and the Spanish. Ridolfi had funded the proposed rebellion of the Roman Catholic northern magnates, headed by the earls of Northumberland and Westmoreland. Ridolfi naively believed that a vast number of Roman Catholics would support the venture. William Cecil, Lord Burleigh's agent, got wind of the plot, which collapsed while Ridolfi was abroad. Norfolk was executed in 1572 and Mary, Queen of Scots was greatly discredited.

1583: *The Throgmorton Plot*

Intention: To assassinate Elizabeth. Supplant her with Mary, Queen of Scots with the help of Spain.

Francis Throgmorton (1554–84), a zealous Roman Catholic, was the player in numerous plots abroad against Elizabeth's government. While organising communications between Mary, Queen of Scots, her agent Thomas Morgan and Spanish ambassador Don Bernardino de Mendoza, Throgmorton was arrested and under torture revealed plans for an invasion from the Spanish Netherlands under the Duke of Guise. The plans were thus thwarted; Mendoza was sent back to Spain and Throgmorton was executed at Tyburn.

1586: The Babington Plot

Intention: To assassinate Elizabeth. The stimulation of a Roman Catholic rising in England in favour of Mary, Queen of Scots, who would be placed on the English throne.

The conspiracy was headed by Anthony Babington (1561–86), one-time page to Mary, Queen of Scots. He formed a secret society to aid and protect Jesuit infiltrators to England and linked up with the Scots queen's emissaries on the Continent. The plot was instigated by the Jesuit priest John Ballard, with Babington as leader and the Pope's blessing. The plot was discovered by Walsingham; Ballard was arrested, racked and executed. Babington tried to save his skin by offering information and fled in disguise; he was captured, held in the Tower of London, indicted and executed in September 1586. A special court found Mary, Queen of Scots, then in English captivity, guilty of treason and she was beheaded at Fotheringay Castle, 8 February 1587.

Why was Charles I executed?

There was such a groan by the thousands then present, as I never heard before and desire I may never hear again.

Contemporary diarist Philip Henry commenting on the crowd's reaction on being shown the severed head of Charles I.

Charles Stuart was crowned King of England at Westminster Abbey on 2 February 1626 and King of Scotland at Holyrood Abbey on 8 June 1633. Like his grandmother, Mary, Queen of Scots, he met his end on the block, being executed at Whitehall Palace, London, on 30 January 1649.

From the first parliament of Charles I's reign in 1625, there began a slow and steady opposition to royal power, both religious and constitutional. It is said that Charles 'hated the very name of Parliament' and he ruled without one for eleven years, 1629–40. Among other things to thwart Parliament, Charles raised money without their leave and ruled with an absolute authority in all matters which he believed was his divine right. When the Civil War of 1642–46 broke out between Charles and Parliament, the death of the monarch was not an original aim. Yet, there was an inevitability about Charles's dire fate as he clashed with MPs over financial, religious and political issues. Relations irretrievably soured when on 4 January 1642 Charles entered the House of Commons with an armed guard to arrest five members. The members had already fled, and civil war became inevitable. The war advances swayed between Royalists and Parliamentarians, until disaster for Charles at the Battle of Naseby, 1645. By 1646 Charles surrendered to the Scots Army who handed him over to the English and Charles was imprisoned.

At length Charles was brought to trial in Westminster Hall, before a tribunal of 135 judges. By the laws of the land the tribunal was illegal and unrepresentative. Charles refused to acknowledge the jurisdiction of the court and refused to enter a plea. Charles was accused of treason by levying war against Parliament. In reality Parliament was as responsible for the Civil War as Charles. Only 53 out of the 135 members of the tribunal attended the court. Charles was found guilty and only 59 of the tribunal members signed the sentence of death. Charles's execution was greeted with a general feeling of public horror. Charles met his end with dignity and courage. Contrary to the stated aims of the Parliamentarians they made Charles into a martyr. Charles's comment that he was going 'from a corruptible to an incorruptible crown' assured his saintly status.

Lucy Hutchinson, wife of the Parliamentarian Governor of Nottingham, Col John Hutchinson, wrote, 'Men wondered that so good a man [as Charles I] should be so bad a king'. She brought into focus for many Puritans the marked differences between Charles's undoubted virtues and his failure in politics. Something of the mindset of Charles I can be seen in *Eikon Basilike: The Pourtraicture of His Sacred Majestie in His Solitudes and Sufferings* compiled, it is thought, by John Gauden (d.1662), Bishop of Worcester. It purported to be the meditations of Charles I based on his own papers. Published in the year of his execution it showed how Charles wanted the world to see him. What Charles emphasised was that, although a sinner who made mistakes, he was answerable only to God and not his subjects. He further emphasised that it was his duty to preserve 'the true doctrine of the Christian faith' as set out by the Church of England. Consequently he was against the denominations of Roman Catholicism and Presbyterianism. For these two tenets Charles was prepared to die. The book became a bestseller with thirty reprints in one year.

Charles had a great love for his family, particularly his wife Henrietta Maria, and possessed great charm, modesty and politeness. He insisted on proper ceremonial and court etiquette, not for his own vanity but for the dignity of his position. Devoutly religious, but not bookish, Charles was described as intellectually weak and lacking in intelligence; certainly the latter was shown in his decisions on political matters. Charles lacked tact and imagination, he was prone to vacillate – promising one thing to one and another to another but never following through – and he was out of touch with public opinion. He also pursued secret plots and intrigues, and tried to be all things to all men. In the end he could have saved his throne and his head if he had agreed to be a 'limited monarch' (as his successor Charles II), with his powers restricted to the will of parliament.

Still today, the anniversary of the execution of Charles I is kept alive by those who believe that Parliament had no right to chop off his head. One, the Royal Martyr Church Union, made up of distant descendants of the Cavaliers, hold a service at St Mary's Episcopal Cathedral, Edinburgh, to mourn his violent death. The liturgy is taken from the King Charles prayer book. Several of their members hope for the return of his bloodline and for the subjugation of Parliament to the Crown. In London the king's execution is remembered by the Society of King Charles the Martyr.

How many attempts were there on Queen Victoria's life?

> If Englishmen may beat their wives,
> It plainly may be seen,
> They must not take the liberty
> To strike the British Queen.
>
> *Pearson Collection of Nineteenth-Century Ballads.*

Despite the regular huffing and puffing by republican groups, Irish agitators, anti-monarchists sheltering within the Liberal Party and the Cromwellian legatees of radical politics, there were eight main attacks and assassination attempts on Queen Victoria during her long reign of sixty-four years.

When Queen Victoria came to the throne in 1837 royal security was at a minimum. Even sixty years later only one policeman was provided for her safety, for instance, when she visited Balmoral. The first attempt on her life occurred at 6 o'clock on the evening of 10 June 1840. Prince Albert and a pregnant Queen Victoria were driving in a low carriage up London's Constitution Hill, after visiting the queen's mother the Duchess of Kent, when the attack occurred. Prince Albert sent this account of the incident to his brother Prince Ernest of Saxe-Coburg:

12 June 1840: I saw a small disagreeable looking man leaning against the rail of Green Park only six paces from us, holding something towards us. Before I could see what it was, a shot cracked out. It was so dreadfully loud that we were both quite stunned. Victoria, who had been looking to the left, towards a rider, did not know the cause of the noise. My first thought was that, in her present state, the fright might harm her. I put both arms around her and asked her how she felt, but she only laughed. Then I turned round to look at the man (the horses were frightened and the carriage stopped). The man stood there in a theatrical position, a pistol in each hand. It seemed ridiculous. Suddenly he stooped, put a pistol on his arm, aimed at us and fired, the bullet must have gone over our heads judging by the hole made where it hit the garden wall.

The attacker was a feeble-minded youngster called Edward Oxford. He was grabbed and held until the police arrested him. A crowd gathered around the royal couple cheering enthusiastically at their escape; it was a miracle that Oxford had missed at such close range. A group of gentlemen on horseback escorted the royal couple back to Buckingham Palace. Oxford was imprisoned at Newgate and tried on a charge of high treason at the Central Criminal Court before Lord Chief Justice Thomas Denman. Defended by Sidney Taylor, Oxford was found 'Guilty but Insane'; he was removed to Bethlehem Hospital for the insane at Moorfields. After thirty-five years he was released and went, under surveillance, to Australia.

In spite of this attack no extra precautions were instituted for Queen Victoria's public or private safety. On Sunday 30 May 1842 a second attack occurred. This time Queen Victoria and Prince Albert were driving along the Mall from the Chapel Royal towards Buckingham Palace. Albert, writing to his father later, said: '[I] saw a man step out from the crowd and present a pistol fully at me. He was some two paces from us ...' Queen Victoria, looking the other way, saw nothing, but Albert heard the trigger click; the shot misfired and the perpetrator disappeared into the crowd.

Behind closed palace doors it was decided to try to identify the culprit by giving him a second chance. It was a curiously foolhardy scheme sanctioned by Prime Minister Robert Peel. The royal couple set off on that Sunday afternoon with Col Charles Arbuthnot and Lt Col William Wylde as outrider equerries. On the return drive from Hampstead, the assassin struck again. As the carriage sped past him the assassin's shot missed and the man was arrested. He was identified as John Francis, a 20-year-old cabinetmaker. Committed to Newgate, he was tried for high treason and found guilty; he was sentenced to be hung, drawn and quartered. On Queen Victoria's authority the sentence was commuted to transportation for life to Norfolk Island. Francis was ultimately released on 'ticket-of-leave' in 1867.

Although she was anxious to have her security increased, on Sunday 3 July 1842, while driving down the Mall from the Chapel Royal with King Leopold I of the Belgians, the 16-year-old John William Bean made to fire a pistol at the carriage. The weapon was knocked from the boy's hand, but he too disappeared into the crowd. The pistol was found to contain a curious mixture of paper, tobacco and gunpowder. The police gathered a description of the boy, who had a noticeable spinal deformity. All males of similar age, who were described as 'hunchbacked', were arrested until Bean was found. Bean was sentenced to eighteen months in prison.

This third attempt on Victoria's life caused the law to be changed. Oxford, Francis and Bean had not been political assassins, but deranged publicity seekers. So the new law backed by Robert Peel provided for 'the further protection and security of her Majesty's person'. It was not now high treason to attack the monarch but a 'high misdemeanour' punishable by up to seven years' transportation or imprisonment, with the options of hard labour and a birching.

On 19 May 1849 Queen Victoria's life was threatened again by a mentally ill Irishman called William Hamilton. His intention was to 'frighten the English Queen with a home-made pistol'. Changing his mind he borrowed a functioning pistol from his landlady and fired a charge at Queen Victoria as she drove down Constitution Hill. The pistol was found to have no bullet in it. Hamilton was transported for seven years.

Robert Pate was bent not on assassination but punishment. On 27 July 1850 the retired lieutenant of the 10th Hussars struck Queen Victoria over the head with a cane as she drove home after visiting her dying uncle Prince Adolphus of Cambridge. As the carriage carrying the queen, the Prince of Wales, Prince Alfred and Princess Alice and lady-in-waiting Fanny Jocelyn, slowed to enter a gate, the escorting equerry was pushed aside by the crowd who had gathered to see the royal party. Pate took his chance. He struck, but was seized by the crowd. Queen Victoria was knocked unconscious, but soon revived to suffer shock, bruising and a headache. Pate too was sentenced to seven years' transportation.

Queen Victoria was informed of a curious threat to her life. On 26 May 1872 a young telegraph clerk called Albert Young appeared before High Court Judge Henry Charles Lopes. Young had sent a letter threatening the life of the queen unless she sent £40 each to some fifty Irish folk who had been dispossessed by their landlords. Young was tried on a charge of intimidation and the bench took a serious view of Young's intent; his sentence after the guilty verdict was ten years' penal servitude.

A weak-minded youth called Arthur O'Connor, nephew of the Chartist leader, the late Fergus O'Connor, took it into his addled head to frighten the queen into authorising the release of Irish Fenian men, then in custody. Towards this end, on 28 February 1872, O'Connor pointed a pistol at her while her carriage paused at the Garden Gate of Buckingham Palace. Prince Arthur jumped out of the carriage to grab the man but was beaten to it by her Highland servant John Brown. Brown was rewarded with a gold medal and a £25 annuity. Prince Arthur received a gold pin in thanks (much to the Prince of Wales's disgust at so paltry a reward when Brown was better favoured). O'Connor was sentenced to a year in prison. Afraid that O'Connor would try to assassinate her on his release Queen Victoria pressed Prime Minister Gladstone to have him deported. In the event O'Connor agreed to a voluntary exile.

As Queen Victoria's carriage stood outside Windsor railway station on 2 March 1882, Roderick McLean fired a pistol at Queen Victoria. Not quite sure what had happened, Queen Victoria was informed by John Brown, who had been riding as postilion, that 'that man fired at Your Majesty's carriage'. Two Eton boys in the crowd ran forward and repeatedly struck McLean with their umbrellas until he was seized by Superintendent George Hayes of the Windsor Police. The Eton boys became the heroes of the hour, and a few days later Queen Victoria 'received 900 Eton boys in the Quadrangle' of their school to thank the two boys personally.

This last attempt on Queen Victoria's life was undoubtedly the most dangerous of all, as McLean's pistol was loaded with six bullets; another firing and McLean might not have missed. McLean was tried at Reading Assizes where he stated that his intent to kill the monarch was to draw public attention to his poverty. He had been awarded the official 6d [3p] a week poor relief but demanded that he should get 10s [50p]; it was all the queen's fault that he had not been paid, he said. McLean was declared by the court not fit to be responsible for his actions and he was sent for treatment at asylums in Weston-Super-Mare and Wells. He was released 'cured' in 1884.

With one exception, none of Queen Victoria's assailants was of mature years, and all showed signs of mental illness. Roderick McLean was declared insane as well as Robert Pate and Edward Oxford; the others were more of the 'half-baked loner' variety than raving lunatics. Had one of them succeeded, the accelerated reign of Edward VII might have completely altered the structure of British monarchy and perhaps the descent into the First World War.

Which monarchs were deemed 'bumped off' by royal doctors?

The King's life is moving peacefully towards its close.
Bulletin drafted by royal doctor Lord Dawson at Sandringham, 1936.

'My dearest husband … passed away on Jan 20th at 5 minutes before midnight.' So wrote Queen Mary as a final postscript to George V's holograph diary which he had kept since 3 May 1880. The nation entered a period of mourning unaware that a royal secret had formed at Sandringham which would have horrified the thirties generation.

This secret was revealed to the public in 1986 when biographer Francis Watson disclosed that physician-in-ordinary Bernard Edward Dawson, Viscount Dawson of Penn (1864–1945), administered a lethal dose of morphine and cocaine into George V's jugular vein at 11.55 p.m. on Monday 20 January 1936. The surrounding publicity of Watson's biography of Dawson caused some controversy: 'Was George V's death treason?' asked the *Independent*. Dawson's reasons for acting the way he did, according to an incredible statement, were so that news of the king's death and his obituaries would be first carried by 'quality' newspapers like *The Times* rather than in the evening or by more downmarket papers. Some historians have averred that Dawson's actions were murder.

Just like her husband, the death of Queen Mary, at 10.35 p.m. on Tuesday 24 March 1953, has been described as a 'mercy killing'. The reason? So that her approaching death would not disrupt the coronation on 2 June of her granddaughter Queen Elizabeth II. Queen Mary's death ten weeks before the coronation assured that the coronation was outside the official mourning period, and so had no need to be postponed. Uncorroborated comment suggests that royal doctors Dawson of Penn and Sir John Weir had discussed the matter with Queen Mary who agreed that her death should not interfere with the coronation plans.

The idea that monarchs were 'bumped off' by royal doctors is not new. Some such instances were moved by politico-religious reasons. On Saturday 7 June 1594, Dr Roderigo Lopez was hung, drawn and quartered at Tyburn Fields after he had been convicted at London's Guildhall of plotting to poison Queen Elizabeth I. While Lopez was a player in the Roman Catholic plots to murder Queen Elizabeth, other doctors were more subtle or cack-handed in ending their monarch's lives.

Charles II died of uraemia, chronic nephritis and syphilis. That's how his death certificate might have read, but in medical history Charles is said to have been murdered by 'iatrogenic regicide'. On Sunday 1 February 1685, the king retired to his chambers with a sore foot to be attended by his physician Sir Edmund King; shortly afterwards the king was struck with an apoplexy. Sir Edmund drew off 'sixteen ounces of blood', risking his own death for treason by not first obtaining the permission of the Privy Council for the bloodletting. Thereafter, as Charles was laid on what would be his deathbed, historian Thomas Babington Macaulay noted that the king was 'tortured like an Indian at the stake'. A total of a dozen doctors now circled Charles's bed. They drew off 'toxic humours' from the king, bled and purged him, shaved his head, applied cantharides plasters and red-hot irons to the skin. For five days, in full view of family, government ministers and hangers-on, Charles was dosed with enemas of rock salt and syrup of buckthorn and an 'orange infusion of metals in white wine'. The king was treated with a horrific cocktail of lethal potions: white hellebore root, Peruvian bark, white vitriol in paeony water, distillation of cowslip flowers, sal ammoniac, julep of black cherry water, oriental bezoar stone from the stomach of a goat and boiled spirits from a human skull. Despite all this the king retained a sense of humour and said to his physicians: 'I am sorry, gentlemen, for being such an unconscionable time a-dying.' Charles's treatment was topped off with 'heart tonics', but to no avail; exhausted, his body raw and aching with the burns and inflammation caused by his doctors, the king lapsed into a coma and died at noon on 7 February 1685.

Queen Anne was a woman of many ills. After her death at Kensington Palace on 1 August 1714, her physician Sir David Hamilton was accused at the autopsy of her body of hastening her death by not spotting, or ignoring, the queen's supposed condition of dropsy. He was not accused of murdering the monarch, but a later sovereign's death was considered to have been 'manipulated'.

Queen Victoria's uncle William IV had a full death certificate of suffering from bronchopneumonia, aortic and mitral valvular disease, myocarditis and syphilis. The king knew he was dying and as Benjamin Disreali reported, 'The King dies like an old Lion'. Following the king's death on Tuesday 20 June 1837, a controversy raged in the medical profession concerning the royal doctors' handling of the king's last days. Each day as the king moved slowly to death medical bulletins were issued. Contemporary doctors considered that royal physicians like Dr William Chambers and Drs James Johnson and William Macmichael had issued bulletins that were mendacious. In them the king was declared not to be terminally ill, and they gave them an optimistic spin. There were those who believed that political pressure had been put on the doctors to play down imminent death. An accusing finger was pointed at William Lamb, Lord Melbourne, the Liberal Prime Minister. Melbourne's cabinet was divided; a general election was due and Melbourne wanted no popular sympathy for the king to be reflected in an increased Tory vote. In the event Melbourne won with a reduced majority. Could future medical bulletins on royal health be trusted again?

Did intruders breach the walls of Buckingham Palace?

INTRUDER AT THE QUEEN'S BEDSIDE

She kept him talking for 10 minutes ... then a footman came to her aid.

Daily Express, *Friday 9 July 1982.*

Since the increased incidence of possible terrorist attacks, new state-of-the-art CCTV cameras and alarms have been installed at Buckingham Palace and the number of armed officers have been increased. A new royal security coordinator post was created for royal palaces when in 2003 comedian Aaron Barschak gatecrashed Prince William's 21st birthday party at Windsor Castle, and newspaper reporter from the *Daily Mirror* Ryan Parry obtained a job as a footman. A series of notorious incidences of intruders at royal palaces have occurred in modern times. For instance, in July 1982, Michael Fagan obtained access to the queen's bedroom, but probably the most incredible Buckingham Palace intruder was during the early years of Queen Victoria's reign.

Around 5 o'clock on the morning of 14 December 1838, gentleman porter at Buckingham Palace, George Cox, was going about his duties when he came across a begrimed boy wandering the corridors. On being challenged the boy fled, but was soon arrested in the Marble Hall. He appeared before Magistrate White. Although he gave his name as Edward Cotton, the 15-year-old was really one Edward Jones, whose father Henry Jones was a tailor in Bell Yard, York Street, Westminster, who had thrown him out for bad behaviour. Jones had worked for a time as a builder's apprentice. His intention in breaching the wall of Buckingham Palace, wherein he had successfully avoided the numerous gentlemen porters, duty constables of the A Division and foot guards, was to see

Queen Victoria at close quarters, sketch the palace's grand staircase, and attend a Privy Council meeting. All this he had done over a period of eleven months, successfully secreting himself in cupboards and empty rooms. He told the magistrate: 'I was obliged to wash my shirt, now and again,' and he lived off 'victuals in the kitchen'. Jones appeared before the magistrate twice on remand for further investigations and was finally to appear at Westminster Sessions on 28 December 1838. His defence lawyer, Mr Prendergast, convinced the jury that Jones's actions were no more than a 'boyish prank' and he was found Not Guilty of a malicious intent to harm the queen.

Edward Jones became something of a celebrity; he was dubbed 'In-I-Go' Jones by the poet Samuel Rogers and was offered a job as a 'turn' on the theatrical stage. Jones turned down the offer.

His thirst for exploring the mysteries of the royal household brought him once more into the public eye. Just after midnight on Thursday 3 December 1840, Queen Victoria's nurse Mrs Lilly was awoken by a noise in the queen's dressing room. She summoned the page Mr Kinnaird and with Queen Victoria's old governess Baroness Lehzen, they discovered Edward Jones under a sofa. This time proceedings against Jones were conducted in private by the Privy Council, who discovered that he had scaled the walls of Buckingham Palace somewhere up Constitution Hill and had entered by a window. He said he had enjoyed sitting in Queen Victoria's throne. Jones was committed to the House of Correction for three months as 'a rogue and a vagabond'. Jones's new case was made much of in the comic papers *The Age*, *The Satirist* and *Punch*. Edward Jones, however, was not finished with his palace escapades.

Jones was given a further three months' detention in March 1841 for planning a new entry to Buckingham Palace. On his release Jones was again arrested; this time he was found in the royal apartments 'enjoying a hearty meal of cold meat and potatoes'.

The newspaper-reading public were amused at Jones's battle of wits with the palace authorities, who had increased security.

The Privy Council took the view that the ease in which Jones entered the palace might tempt an assassin to emulate the boy. Jones was given a further three-month sentence, this time with hard labour.

Jones's escapades became a political football to annoy Prime Minister Lord Melbourne. Something had to be done about Jones once and for all. In the end, after official bungling in order to get him a berth, Edward Jones was 'sent to sea' and nothing more was heard of him.

Quaint, Quirky, Crowns and Coronations

Why was George III called 'Farmer George'?

The King rode with me for two and a half hours, talking farming and reasoning upon points ... His farm is in admirable order, and crops all clean and fine ...

Arthur Young (1741–1820), editor of Annals of Agriculture *(1748–1809).*

G eorge III's nickname 'Farmer George' is well known. The king's interest in agriculture is hardly surprising, for the majority of his subjects were employed in agriculture. From the reign of Henry I there was hunting parkland around Windsor Castle. By the 1780s George III brought Windsor Castle back to life after some fifty years of neglect. As George was, as author Michael De-la-Noy has pointed out, 'far better fitted for the role of country squire than that of king', he expressed his interest in agriculture by developing Windsor Castle's parklands. He had the land at Lower Park (Datchet, or Mastrick Meadows) and Upper Park (Frogmore side) surveyed for agricultural possibilities, and particularly at Frogmore farm he indulged his bent in overseeing the husbandry with the help of the manager Mr Kent. Here George incorporated the farming methods pioneered in Holland and Norfolk and developed a dairy. Even so George took almost daily pleasure in inspecting his three farms at Windsor which covered in excess of 1,000 acres. He created them in Windsor Great Park and his enthusiasm for them assured that they ran at a profit. George's academic knowledge of farming sheep, botany and agriculture in general was thorough. Acting on the advice of President of the Royal Society, Sir Joseph Banks, he imported sheep from Spain. His sheep farming acted out a key role in the breeding of sheep which laid down the ancestor strains from Australia and New Zealand's Merino sheep. It may be noted on a more domestic level that George III and Queen Charlotte were the first to import the (German) Christmas tree to England, but it was Prince Albert who popularised it nationwide.

George III wrote letters to the publication *Annals of Agriculture* on farming practices under the pen name of Ralph Robinson, the name of one of his shepherds. He kept up-to-date with all the latest developments in agriculture and animal husbandry. When Captain Cook set off in *Endeavour* in 1769, the king asked Cook to take with him a number of his farm animals to stock new herds in Polynesia.

The man in the street looked upon George III's love of farming as comical. His agricultural interests gave great scope to the cartoonists of the day who lampooned him as 'Farmer George'. The popular caricaturist James Gillray set society laughing with such depictions of George as 'alarming a cottager at Windsor by his persistent questioning and close inspection'. Gillray also portrayed George and Queen Charlotte in country farming garb riding home to the castle from a country fair. George was satirised as well in words. John Wolcot (Peter Pindar) offered the public the scenario of George hobnobbing with a farm labourer's wife as to how an apple gets into an apple dumpling. George had the habit of adding 'What! What!' to everything he said so Wolcot used that too in the apple dumpling skit:

> In tempting row the naked dumplings lay,
> When lo! the monarch in his usual way,
> Like lightening spoke, 'What's this? what's this? what? what?'
> 'No!' cried the staring monarch with a grin,
> 'How? how? the devil got the apple in?'

Why does Queen Elizabeth II have corgis?

Have a footman enter with a silver tray each afternoon. On it should be: a jug of gravy, a plate of dog biscuits, a bowl of dog food and three spoons.

> *Queen Elizabeth II's advice on the care of corgis, as noted by Craig Brown and Lesley Cunliffe (1982).*

In 1933, when she was 7 years old, her father King George VI (then Duke of York) gave Princess Elizabeth her first corgi. Thereafter the dog, and subsequent additions, became a part of her life. As a general rule visitors and staff are wary of the dogs. The princess's nanny, Marion Crawford, remembered how one corgi, Dookie, 'took a piece out of Lord Lothian's hand'. His lordship dismissed the incident as 'nothing'. 'All the same,' said the princess, 'he bled all over the floor.' Wherever she went, even on honeymoon, the princess, and then as queen, took the corgi too, whether by car or aircraft of the Queen's Flight.

In 2006 the queen chartered the vessel *Hebridean Princess* for a tour around the coast of Scotland as part of her 80th birthday celebrations. The company owning the vessel had a strict no dogs policy. As part of the £125,000 charter, the queen insisted that the ban be lifted to accommodate her beloved corgis – it was. Over the years the queen has had in excess of thirty corgis, and in 2007 the tally was five: Emma, Linnet, Monty, Holly and Willow.

More than one courtier has expressed the opinion that to Queen Elizabeth dogs are the 'real love of her life' – along with horses.

The queen is following a long tradition of royal 'pet keeping'. The chronicler Goscelin, writing in the *Life of St Edith* (*c*.1080) about Princess Edith (d.984), the daughter of Edgar I of the House of Cedric and Denmark, noted that she cared for a personal 'suburb' (i.e. precinct) of native and foreign animals at Wilton Nunnery, which had been founded by Ealhswith (d.902), queen of Alfred the Great. The animals may have been gifts to the princess and her mother Queen Athelfleda, Abbess of Wilton. Perhaps this was the first zoological collection in England. Nevertheless, a collection of wild animals for court pleasure and display began when Henry I maintained his menagerie in his park at Woodstock, near Oxford. His animals included lions, camels and a porcupine, gifted to him by brother monarchs.

Royal pets have been immortalised in paintings and photographs. Van Dyck portrayed the five children of Charles I in 1637, with the Prince of Wales (later Charles II) leaning his arm on the head of a huge dog. Queen Victoria spent regular sums on having her animals photographed. For example, in 1854 photographer William Bambridge took about a month to photograph the royal dogs; his bill for the mounted album was £25.19*s* (£25.95*s* is about £1,650 today). Queen Victoria also pioneered the royal animal memorial. When her beloved King Charles spaniel Dash died in 1840, the dog, a gift from her mother the Duchess of Kent and which had been painted in oils by Edwin Landseer, was given this epitaph:

His attachment was without selfishness,

His playfulness without malice,

His fidelity without deceit.

Reader, if you would live beloved and die regretted, profit by the example of Dash.

When Queen Victoria married Prince Albert, his German greyhound Eos went with them on honeymoon. Victoria had Eos painted by Landseer in a portrait she gave Albert as a Christmas present in 1841. Eos died in 1844 and was buried in Windsor Castle Home Park; a statue, based on the Landseer portrait, was erected in memory of the dog. The policies of all Queen Victoria's homes were bespotted with the graves of her pets. As her journals, photographs and portraits show, Queen Victoria favoured dachshunds, pomeranians and collies. When she showed interest in the latter breed the collie became fashionable; so much so that the dog's photographs were sold as *cartes de visite*.

Kennels were built in Windsor Home Park in 1840–41 and at any one time the queen had upwards of 100 dogs. When Edward VII succeeded to the throne in 1903 he had the kennels moved to Sandringham. Perhaps Edward VII's most famous dog was Caesar, a terrier bred by the Duchess of Newcastle. A mischievous dog that had disdain for all but the king; it went with him everywhere from Balmoral to Biarritz. He was even immortalised as a Carl Fabergé jewelled chalcedony figurine; Caesar sported a specially made collar with the inscription: 'I am Caesar. I belong to the king.' In 1910 Caesar won international fame when he walked behind the coffin at the monarch's funeral procession.

Today the queen remains one of the most famous breeders of Pembroke corgis in the world, each dog sharing the bloodline of her first corgi, Susan. Thus corgis and royalty now go together.

Who was Britain's first royal car owner?

[John Montague as driver in] April 1902 is notable as being the first time a reigning monarch of England [*sic*] had been driven in a motor-car.

Lord Montague, The Motoring Montagues.

The motor car had many detractors as 'dirty' and 'evil' when Albert Edward, Prince of Wales, had his first drive. Called the 'autocar', or 'horseless carriage' in its early form, the machine caught the prince's imagination when at 55 he had his first drive on 14 February 1896 at the Imperial Institute, South Kensington. The vehicle was a Cannstall-Daimler and the driver was The Hon. Evelyn Ellis, cousin of the prince's equerry Gen Sir Arthur Ellis. The car had rubber-tyred carriage wheels, carriage lamps, flat mudguards and a large leather hood. Steering was the 'tiller' type and the engine was mid-mounted. A second demonstration by Daimler took place in the grounds of Buckingham Palace on 27 November 1897. The prince's first drive on public roads was in June 1898 when he visited the Earl of Warwick at Warwick Castle. A fleet of Daimlers took the royal party to Compton Verney, the home of Lord Willoughby de Broke. The prince bought his first Daimler in the early part of 1900; this had the Model A frame with a twin-cylinder 6hp engine with bodywork by Hoopers of London. The prince was taught to drive by Oliver Stanton (who had taught him to cycle). By 1905 the now King Edward had purchased seven Daimlers. In 1904 Queen Alexandra became the first crowned queen of Great Britain to own a car; in this year she took delivery of a 24hp Wolseley landaulette.

Did King John lose the Crown Jewels?

King John lost his Crown in the Wash.

Schoolboy 'laundry joke', nineteenth century.

John Lackland, King of England from 6 April 1199 to 18 October 1216, the youngest son of Henry II and Eleanor of Aquitaine, is probably best remembered today for being forced to sign the Magna Carta (Great Charter) by rebel barons at Runnymede on 15 June 1215. Harshly blackened as an 'evil king' in the Robin Hood myths, John did create a whole raft of enemies and it was during the last civil war of his reign that he is believed to have lost his treasure and the Crown Jewels.

King John had a great liking for jewellery and the loss of his treasure greatly grieved him. Chroniclers note that his treasure chest included:

> ... a clasp ornamented with emeralds and rubies, given him by the Bishop of Norwich, four rings of emerald, sapphire, garnets and topaz, presented to him by Pope Innocent III, 143 cups of white silver, a wand of gold with a cross given him by the Knights Hospitaller and the regalia which his grandmother Matilda wore when she was crowned Empress.

How did John manage to lose his treasure?

During the last civil war, John successfully took Cambridge from the rebel barons and rode through Huntingdonshire and Lincolnshire to subdue eastern England. After recovering from dysentery at Kings Lynn, he led his army south-west to Wisbech on 11 October 1216. His target was Swineshead Abbey. To achieve his goal he had to cross the Wellstream (the old River Ouse), which flowed into the Wash. As his soldiers advanced the baggage train containing supplies, armaments, the royal treasure and the Crown Jewels lumbered behind. The intention was to traverse the 4½ mile-wide mouth of the Wellstream (now much further inland than it is today) at low tide. In the autumn fenland mist the wagons lost their way, became entrapped in quicksand and were stuck as the tides rushed in. The chronicler Roger of Wendover in his *Flores Historiarum* noted, 'the ground was opened in the midst of the waves, and bottomless whirlpools engulfed everything, together with men and horses, so that not a single foot-soldier got away to bear tidings of the disaster to the king'. Dog-tired and wracked with dysentery, John died two days later at Newark Castle; he was 48.

Biographer of John, Professor W.L. Warren, has a cautionary comment for those who would 'treasure hunt' John's possessions. He quotes the story of how a priest, who went to Newark Castle to say the requiem mass for John, told Ralph, Abbot of Coggeshall, 'that he had seen men leaving the city laden with loot'. Whether John lost his treasures and Crown Jewels in the Wash, or was robbed of them on his deathbed, remains a mystery. Only one thing is certain: identifiable artefacts from such an event have never ever turned up.

Does Scotland have its own Crown Jewels?

Uneasy lies the head that wears a crown.

> *William Shakespeare,* King Henry IV, *Part 2, I, ii.*

With eight of Scotland's monarchs murdered – nine if you include Mary, Queen of Scots – many a Scots monarch's head has lain uneasy. Yet there are no finer symbols of Scotland's monarchy and feelings of independence and nationhood than its crown regalia.

The Crown Jewels of Scotland are known as The Honours of Scotland and comprise three main artefacts.

The Crown: The foundation is the circlet of gold which is said to come from the helmet of Robert I, the Bruce, and which he wore at the Battle of Bannockburn, 24 June 1314. Bruce was crowned with the circlet in 1306. Surmounted by four golden arches and topped with a blue enamel celestial globe, the crown was altered for James V in 1540. This is the oldest crown of the British regalia. It is known that King John Baliol had a set of regalia but this was taken away from him by Edward I when he made Baliol his puppet ruler. The extant crown is set with carbuncles, jacinths, rod crystals, topazes, amethysts, diamonds and pearls. All these enclose a crimson bonnet.

The Sceptre: Presented to James IV in 1491 by Pope Alexander VI. It was remodelled for James V in 1536.

The Sword of State: Of all these elements it is perhaps the Sword of State that has had the most adventurous life. During 2007 a special reception took place at the Palace of Holyrood to mark the 500th anniversary of the coming of the sword to Scotland. It was a gift to James IV from Giuliano della Rovere, known to history as Pope Julius II. During a celebration of solemn High Mass at the Abbey of Holyrood on Easter Sunday 1507 the sword was presented by *cavaliere* Antonio Inviziati, on behalf of the Pope.

The 1.4m steel-bladed sword was crafted by Italian cutler Domenico Da Sutri and came with a wooden scabbard covered with red velvet and a belt of silk and gold. The overall decorative design is based on the heraldic arms of Pope Julius II – oak tree, leaves and acorns, plus dolphins; the former representing the risen Christ and the latter his church. On the blade, which has been broken in two at some time in history, appear the figures of St Peter and St Paul on alternate sides; beneath each are the letters JULIUS II

PONT[IFEX] MAX[IMUS] for 'Julius II, Supreme Pontiff'. With the sword came a consecrated hat of dark crimson velvet, lined with ermine. This too had symbolic designs of an embroidered gold dove decorated with pearls to signify the Holy Spirit.

From medieval times the Honours were kept at Edinburgh Castle to be produced for state occasions and for coronations. It seems they were first used together at the coronation of Mary, Queen of Scots at the Chapel Royal, Stirling Castle, 9 September 1543. Cardinal David Beaton, Archbishop of St Andrews placed the crown symbolically on the head of the weeks old infant and guided her tiny hand around the shaft of the sceptre and wrapped the belt of the Sword of State around her waist. The Honours appeared again at the coronations of James VI at the Holy Rude church, Stirling, 29 July 1567, Charles I at Holyrood, 18 June 1633, and the impromptu coronation of Charles II at Scone on 1 January 1651.

For safekeeping, after Charles II's coronation in what was now Cromwell's occupation of Scotland, the regalia was moved to Dunottar Castle, near Stonehaven, the stronghold of the Earl Marischal of Scotland. The castle was besieged by Cromwellian troops for eight months, but before its surrender the regalia was spirited away by two courageous women, Mrs George Ogilvy of Barras, wife of the Governor of Dunottar and Mrs Christian Granger, wife of the Revd James Granger, minister of nearby Kinneff, aided by a servant girl. Until the Restoration in 1660 the regalia lay buried among some pews at Kinneff church. Incandescent that the regalia was missing, the Cromwellian commander ordered the castle governor Sir George Ogilvy and his wife to be vigorously interviewed into revealing where the regalia was. They never disclosed the secret location although Mrs Ogilvy died of her treatment. In Charles II's reign the regalia were back in Edinburgh Castle to be produced for sittings of the Scottish parliament. When this was dissolved on the Act of Union of 1707 a pledge was made that the regalia should never leave Scotland and they were locked away in an oak chest in the castle where they remained 'lost' for a century.

By the 1800s rumours circulated that the regalia had long been sent to England. Sir Walter Scott was one who believed that a search should be made for them. The chest was located, but could only be unlocked by Royal Warrant. Sir Walter persuaded the Prince Regent, later George IV, to grant the warrant and on 4 February 1819 the chest was opened. Sir Walter described the scene:

> The blows of the hammer echoed with a deep hollow sound ... even those whose expectations had been most sanguine felt at the moment the probability of disappointment ... The joy was therefore extreme when the ponderous lid of the chest being forced open, at the expense of some time and labour, the Regalia was discovered lying at the bottom covered with linen cloths, exactly as they had been left in the year 1707 ... The discovery was instantly announced by running up the Royal Standard above the Castle, to the shouts of the garrison and the multitude assembled on Castle Hill.

The Honours of Scotland are on permanent public display in the Crown Room of Edinburgh Castle, where they have rested since 1617 (apart from during the Cromwellian adventures and when they were hidden in the castle's King David's Tower, 1941–45). They play a pivotal role in Scottish constitutional life. They were formally presented to Elizabeth II (Elizabeth I in Scotland) at St Giles's Kirk, Edinburgh, on 24 June 1953, following the sovereign's London coronation; and they would appear in a similar role for future coronations. The crown alone has been present at the state openings of the Scottish parliament since the first of 1999. Thereat the crown is carried by the Hereditary Keeper of the Palace of Holyroodhouse, the Duke of Hamilton and Brandon.

Who stole the Crown Jewels?

> Blood that wears treason in his face,
> Villain complete in parson's gown,
> How muche he is at court in grace
> For stealing Ormond and the crown!
> Since loyalty does no man good,
> Let's steal the King, and outdo Blood.
>
> *Satirical verse on Colonel Thomas Blood (c. 1618–80).*

At one time the Crown Jewels were housed in Westminster Abbey, and it was 'one of the biggest burglaries in the history of crime', wrote Lewis Broad, that caused them to be transferred to the Tower of London. It was Edward the Confessor who granted the Abbey of St Peter at Westminster the privilege of housing the national regalia. The Crown Jewels were kept in the crypt of the Chapter House, a place secured by a huge double door locked with seven great keys. Herein too, was the wealth in jewels and coin of the Norman kings, who held the Benedictine monks of Westminster in great favour.

Before setting out for campaigns in the north in 1303, King Edward I accumulated a large sum of money in this strongroom. As he rested at Linlithgow, Scotland, a messenger appeared to tell him that the strongroom had been breached and a large part of the contents removed. On Edward's orders Father Wenlock, Abbot of Westminster was arrested, along with forty-eight monks, and thrown into the Tower. The Lord Mayor of London and the Master of the Wardrobe were put in charge of the investigation. The king was now assured that his diadem was safe, but his wealth had vanished. After some two years' of investigation the Sub-Prior and Sacrist were found guilty of the robbery, along with a merchant called Richard de Podlicote. Their fate is not known, but Edward I ordered that the Crown Jewels should now go to the Tower of

London to be housed there in perpetuity. Even so, the Crown Jewels were not entirely safe.

The issue of 8–11 May 1671 of the *London Gazette* gave an account of perhaps the most outrageous robbery of the seventeenth century:

> This morning about seven of the clock, four men coming to Mr. Edwards, Keeper of the Jewel House in the Tower, desired to see the Regal Crown remaining in his custody, he carries them into the room where they were kept, and shows them; but according to the villainous design they it seems came upon, immediately they clap a gag of a strange form into the old man's mouth; who making what noise and resistance he could, they stabbed him a deep wound in the belly with a stilleto [a dagger with a narrow blade], adding several other dangerous wounds on the head with a small beetle [heavy wooden mallet] they had with them, as is believed, to beat together and flatten the Crown, to make it the more easily portable; which having, together with the Ball [i.e. Orb], put into Bags, they had to that purpose brought with them; they fairly walked out, leaving the old man grovelling on the ground, gagged and pinioned ...

The leader of this gang was one Thomas Blood whom the *London Gazette* dubbed 'that notorious traytor and incendary'.

Thomas Blood was born around 1618 at Sarney, Dunboyne, County Meath, Ireland. From a Protestant landowning family Blood began his military career fighting for the Royalists during the Roman Catholic rebellion in Ireland. In 1646 a peace treaty was agreed between the Roman Catholics under Sir Phelim O'Neill and the Royalist James Butler, 12th Earl of Ormonde, which was unacceptable to many devout Protestants and Thomas Blood switched sides from Royalists to Parliamentarians. Thus he went to England to fight alongside his new comrades. In 1649 he was back in Ireland with Cromwell's troops. When Ireland was subjugated, Thomas Blood was rewarded with confiscated lands and a position as JP. Returning to England, Blood married Maria, daughter of Parliamentarian Col John Holcroft in 1650. Following the Restoration of 1660, Blood was involved in the religious struggles in Ireland for the Nonconformist cause. Thus Blood was involved in the 1663 plot to kidnap Charles II's new Lord Lieutenant of Ireland, the Duke of Ormonde, from Dublin Castle. The plot was discovered. Blood fled in disguise to England to be a player in a number of escapades, which included an attack on the Tower of London and plots to murder Charles II and his brother, the devoutly Roman Catholic Duke of York. A backer of some of these schemes was George Villiers, 2nd Duke of Buckingham, who was violently opposed to any Roman Catholic succession through the Duke of York. Throughout, Thomas Blood, who now called himself Colonel Blood, evaded arrest and punishment and 1671 saw the beginnings of his boldest plot yet; to steal the new Crown Jewels which had replaced those ancient pieces sold off by Oliver Cromwell. These were under the protection of The Keeper of the Jewel House, Sir Gilbert Talbot, at the Martin Tower, Tower of London. As he did not live in the Tower, the day to day responsibility for the jewels fell to a septuagenarian assistant keeper, one Talbot Edwards. Edwards had the perk of charging visitors a fee to view the jewels.

Even though security for the Crown Jewels was a shadow of what it is now the breaching of the Tower of London was no mean feat in the seventeenth century. Huge walls, a deep moat, a battalion of the King's Guards and a squad of the Yeomen of the Guard would all have to be evaded. Carefully Blood noted the comings and goings of the Tower's civilian and military staff, most of the former going about their business unchallenged. The Crown Jewels were not directly guarded. A few weeks before the robbery, Blood surveyed the immediate location of the Jewel House dressed as a clergyman paying his visitor's fee and being accompanied by a young actress called Jenny Blame, who threw a bogus faint to distract the assistant keeper and his wife while Blood made his detailed examination. Over a period of time Blood ingratiated himself with the Edwards's.

Blood set out to act on 9 May 1671 and on that day visited the Tower with his son (alias Tom Hunt) and two known criminals Robert Perrott and Richard Halliwell. Outside was William Smith waiting with horses. Taking the 'visitors' to the Jewel House, Edwards was assaulted and bundled up in a cloak, his struggles causing a severe beating. He was stabbed in an attempt to keep him quiet. Blood selected the pieces he wished to steal and made to leave. Aroused from his state of shock Edwards shouted 'Treason! Murder! The Crown is stolen!' as the robbers fled. Now pursued by Edwards's son and a visitor Captain Martin Beckman, the robbers made to escape in the crowd outside the Tower, but they were caught and arrested.

Over the centuries historians have tried to fathom out Blood's motives in stealing the jewels. Could it be financial gain? This was considered unlikely as Blood's other exploits had never included personal monetary profit. Was the capturing of the crown the opening gambit of a plot to depose Charles II? And was the ambitious Duke of Buckingham behind it all? Buckingham believed that through his Plantagenet ancestors (through his mother's family) he had a right to the throne. All in all the theft was probably a political gesture. Triumphing over the authorities would have been a piece of fine propaganda to draw attention to the cause of the Protestant Nonconformists in Ireland. Or, was it a piece of bravado to feed Blood's ego and a 'see what I can do' recklessness?

Whatever the motive, Blood seems to have lived a charmed life. He talked his way out of punishment and remarkably found favour with Charles II at court, being granted a pension of £500 per annum. This caused some suspicion in court circles with the supposition that Charles II used Blood as a spy on the Nonconformists. Blood died on 24 August 1680 to be buried at

New Chapel, Tothill Fields, London. Such was his reputation for trickery that many thought he had feigned death as a ruse to vanish; his body was even dug up to make sure he had died. Yet, whatever the truth about the Thomas Blood Crown Jewels incident, thereafter greater precautions were made to secure their safety.

Which king was the first to have a crown?

> A crown! What is it?
> It is to bear the miseries of a people!
> To hear the murmurs
> Feel their discontents,
> And sink beneath a load of splendid care.
>
> *Hannah More (1745–1833), 'Daniel', Part VI.*

It is a matter of some controversy among historians as to whether or not the early Saxon kings wore a head covering during their coronations. Some say they wore a ceremonial helmet. It is now generally believed that the first king to have a crown at his coronation was Edward the Elder, King of the West Saxons, who ruled 899–924. His coronation took place around 8 June 900 at Kingston-upon-Thames, and was conducted by Plegmund, Archbishop of Canterbury. The second son of Alfred the Great, Edward, probably at his coronation, proclaimed himself as 'by the gift of God's grace, King of the Anglo-Saxons', the first use of the title. At his death at Farndon, in Mercia, on 17 July 924, Edward had fulfilled the new symbolism of his coronation by building on the foundations laid by his father Alfred to create a new Kingdom of England from the English Channel deep into English Northumberland as far as the Firth of Forth.

Which king first adopted the title 'King of England'?

> There was not English armour left,
> Nor any English thing,
> When Alfred came to Athelney
> To be an English king.
>
> *'Ballad of the White Horse', Gilbert Keith*
> *Chesterton (1874–1936).*

Over the years historians have argued which king qualified as the first to be dubbed 'King of All England'. Three kings have been so identified:

1. Egbert of Wessex (r. 802–39); one charter is known to exist which gives him the title *Rex Anglorum* (King of the English), although his rule of Northumbria and East Anglia was tenuous.

2. Alfred the Great (r. 871–99); he accepted sovereignty of the entire kingdom, so he was King of England, but was never crowned as such.

3. Edward the Elder (r. 899–924); Alfred's eldest surviving son was crowned King of England in 901.

Athelstan (r. 924–27), of course, called himself King of the English. However, it may be remembered that at his coronation on 25 January 1603, James I/VI was proclaimed as 'King of England, Scotland, France and Ireland, Defender of the Faith'.

Who was the last British king to lead his troops into battle?

His Majesty was all the Time in the Heat of the Fire; but is in perfect Health.

John Carteret, Earl Granville (1690–1763) to Thomas Pelham-Holles, 1st Duke of Newcastle (1693–1768), The Gentleman's Magazine.

Elector George Augustus of Hanover ruled Great Britain as George II on the death of his father George I on 11 June 1727 until his own death at Kensington Palace, 25 October 1760. On 27 June 1743 he commanded and led his troops onto the battlefield at Dettingen, Bavaria; the site being the north bank of the River Main some 70 miles east of Frankfurt and 3 miles west of Aschaffenburg. This was during the Austrian Succession War 1740–48, caused by Prussia's rejection of the Pragmatic Sanction wherein the rights of Maria Theresa to succeed to the Habsburg throne of her father Emperor Charles VI were enshrined. France also repudiated the sanction.

George II gathered a 52,000-strong national army of British, Dutch and Hanoverian troops, with pro-Austrian German allies, and mustered on the lower Rhine; support was given by the infantry led by John Dalrymple, 2nd Earl of Stair. George advanced slowly into the Main and Necker valleys; meanwhile a 60,000-strong French force under Adrien Maurice, 3rd Duke of Noailles (d.1766) moved into position to block the advance. With tactical skill Noailles virtually blockaded George's force in the Main defiles. His Hanoverian stubbornness to the fore, George extricated his army from the situation, but the initial French cavalry charge of Comte de Grammont almost overwhelmed the allies. 'Now boys,' shouted George, 'now for the honour of England; fire and behave bravely and the French will soon run.' George's horse bolted, however, and threw him; he walked back to the front saying: 'I can be sure of my own legs. They will not run away with me.'

As the day closed George's force held the field, and Noailles retreated after the French Black Musketeers were decimated by the Royal Dragoons, and the French Household Cavalry were routed by the Scots Greys. Some 5,000 French were killed, wounded or taken prisoner, with British losses at around 265 dead and 560 wounded. This was the last occasion on which a British sovereign commanded an army on the battlefield. To commemorate the victory Georg Friedrich Handel composed his *Dettingen Te Deum*.

(Richard III was the last English king to die in battle at Bosworth Field in 1485. Edward, Prince of Wales (later Edward VIII) served as a staff officer in the First World War but was not allowed to fight on the front line. In 1916 he was visited in France at the HQ of His Majesty's Brigade of Guards by his brother Prince Albert (later George VI). On 31 May 1916 Prince Albert was present on board HMS *Collingwood* at the Naval Battle of Jutland when his vessel came under fire; *Collingwood* suffered no casualties.)

Which queen pretended to be invisible?

It was so clear and solitary, it did one good as one gazed around; and the pure mountain air was most refreshing. All seemed to breathe freedom and peace, and to make one forget the world and its sad turmoils.

Queen Victoria, journal entry, September 1848.

Queen Victoria first took up residence at Balmoral Castle in 1848; in 1852 the queen and Prince Albert bought the castle with ambitious plans to rebuild. Although she always held the castle dear as another tribute to Prince Albert's design skills, it was the Scottish countryside she loved best. In particular she had a passion for the shiels and bothies.

The former are huts or cottages – originally shepherd's summer shelters – the latter the name of a cottage used in common by farm labourers. Over the years she refurbished, rebuilt, or built several such dwellings on her estate and often went to them to enjoy the 'wilderness around [them] that beckoned her'. From their windows she could see the tracks that wound away into the distant heather hills and the forests that reminded Prince Albert of the Thuringian Forest of his native Coburg. The shiels and bothies were the gateways to the privacy that the queen longed for and needed. Courtiers noted that when she went out walking on her estate the protocol was that folk 'had to pretend not to see her'. In her illusion of privacy – her attendants were never far away – she pretended to be invisible. When abroad she tried to be incognito, travelling under a pseudonym like the 'Countess of Balmoral'; no one was fooled hailing her with 'Vive la Reine d'Angleterre' or 'Viva la Reina d'Inghilterra'.

Which queen is buried under a railway platform?

Goaded by much mutual encouragements, the whole island rose under the leadership of Boudicca, a lady of royal descent …

Roman orator Publius Cornelius Tacitus (c. 55–120), Annals.

Boudicca, or Boadicea, Queen of the Iron Age tribe the Iceni, led a famous revolt against Roman rule in Britain in AD 60, sacking Londinium (London), Verulamium (St Albans) and Camulodunum (Colchester), throwing the Roman province into chaos. She was finally defeated by Provincial Governor Suetonius Paulinus at a place, the location of which historians still cannot agree, ranging from Mancetter in Warwickshire to Gop Hill, Flintshire.

Historian Dio Cassius tells us that she 'fell sick and died', while Tacitus says she took poison after her defeat. However she died, Dio says that she was given a costly funeral by her people; but where is she buried? Again this is in dispute, but curiously it has long been suggested that she was buried in a grave where Kings Cross Station, London, now stands, while some even narrow down the site to Platform 8.

Was King Richard III really a hunchbacked monster?

He left such a reputation behind him that even his birth was said to have proclaimed him a monster.

James Gairdner (1828–1912), History of the Life and Reign of Richard III.

John Rous (d.1491), the Warwickshire cleric and antiquary was not the first to curry royal favour with his writings. Yet his *Historia Regum Angliae* is said to bear much of the blame for promoting the Tudor myth that Richard III was a 'crook back'. Rous wrote:

Richard was born [2 October 1452] at Fotheringhay in Northampton-shire, retained within his mother's womb for two years and emerging with teeth and hair on his shoulders.

This was clearly nonsense but historians have been thwarted concerning Richard's appearance for there is no contemporary description of him. Yet, look at the portrait of Richard (artist unknown) in the National Portrait Gallery; apart from a rather absent-minded expression, there is no sign of deformity, nor is there in the *c.*1520 copy of the portrait of Richard (possibly when he was the Duke of Gloucester) in the collection of the Society of Antiquaries of London. Both must have appeared in Tudor times but neither show the anti-Richard propaganda of the Tudor court.

The sixth and youngest son of Edmund of Langley, Duke of York and his wife Cecily Neville, it is likely that the 37-year-old duchess had a difficult birth with Richard. As Shakespeare wrote in King Henry VI, Part III: 'For I have often heard my mother say I came into the world with my legs forward.'

Following the description of Richard's birth by Sir Thomas More in his *The History of King Richard the Third* – remembering that More was one of Richard's foremost character assassins – Shakespeare is probably describing a breech birth. The discovery and confirmation of the remains of Richard III, during 4 September 2012 and 4 February 2013, at the site of the now vanished medieval Greyfriars (Franciscan) monastery at Leicester, show that he suffered from severe scoliosis (spinal curvature) and was thus (inappropriately) dubbed 'hunchback'. Also he did not have a 'withered arm' as asserted by More. To the medieval mind, deformity was a mark of being born, if not evil, at the very least of dubious character only a step away from being a creature of witchcraft. It was easy therefore for Tudor detractors like Rous, More and Polydore Vergil to use the superstition of the day concerning deformity to blacken Richard's character, especially when linking him to the murder of his nephews, 'The Princes in the Tower'.

Which king joined a sex club?

It is with these lusty monks of Pittenweem, and their guardian Knights Templar of the Dreel, that the Society or Brotherhood of the Beggar's Benison undoubtedly had its origin. Its motto is the monkish blessing 'Be fruitful and multiply'.

Col M.R. Canch Kavanagh, Résumé of the History of the Order.

Present-day Anstruther, on the south coast of Fife overlooking the Firth of Forth, is made up of two historic settlements: Anstruther Easter and Anstruther Wester divided by a burn known as The Dreel. Long famous for its prosperous maritime traditions, the Burgh of Anstruther west of The Dreel was granted a Royal Charter by James VI on 21 October 1587. By The Dreel's mouth there stood a now vanished castle known as the Castle of Dreel, once the home of the influential Anstruther family.

In a room of the castle met the gentleman's club of The Most Ancient and Puissant Order of the Beggar's Benison and Merryland. Primarily it was a dining club but its fundamental interests were erotic in nature with phallicism of great interest. Records show that it was founded in 1732, while some suggest an earlier medieval provenance. Two main stories persist. Out in the Firth of Forth is the Isle of May and on it, in his monastery, St Adrian was slain by marauding Vikings around AD 870. Adrian's tomb was soon considered to have miraculous powers wherein pagan fertility rites became attached to his Christian shrine and barren women flocked here to be made fertile. James IV of Scots and his Queen Margaret came here to receive the blessing of the Augustinian Prior, 'Be fruitful and multiply'. Thus the Club had its roots.

The Club, too, was long associated with the (apocryphal) tale of how James V of Scots, nicknamed 'the Gudeman of Ballangeich', a pseudonym he used when travelling, came to Anstruther and was unable to cross The Dreel. A local 'buxom gaberlunzie [i.e. beggar] lass' hitched up her skirts and carried the monarch piggy-back over the burn so he could continue his journey to the Castle of Dreel. In recompense James V gave the woman a gold sovereign. She curtseyed to him and gave him her benison:

> May your purse ne'er be toom [empty]
> And you horn aye in bloom.

That night James V dined at the Castle of Dreel and supposedly initiated the Club. Be all that as it may, the Club (which referred to itself as the Order and their members as Knights), met twice a year at Candlemas (February) and St Andrews's Day (30 November), in a room of the Castle of Dreel which they called The Temple. (When the castle was no longer habitable they met at a nearby inn.) In 1738 the members devised a seal with its device a purse of money hanging from a phallus with the anchor of Anstruther's arms in the background. At this time membership cost ten guineas (£10.50), a diploma of membership three guineas (£3.15) and a gold medal to wear five guineas (£5.25). The membership was headed by a 'Sovereign', and several local notables held the office from 'Sir' John McNaughton, Collector of Customs at Anstruther to 'Sir' John Lumisdaine, a local estate owner. The 'Sovereign's' deputy was the 'Remembrancer', with a 'Chaplain' added in 1767. The membership was composed of thirty-two 'Knights' and the founder members were all from this part of the country known as the East Neuk of Fife; its membership included landowners and merchants, smugglers and peers as well as Jacobites, Whigs, Presbyterians and Episcopalians.

The main meeting was held on 30 November with a dinner, with an initiation for new members to follow; the whole ethos of the meeting has been described as 'the pagan glorification of the phallus and the puerile initiation ceremony concerning its display and measuring'. Thereafter a new member was toasted in wine from glasses engraved with the Club Seal of the Order. The toast was 'To the beggar maid and joy'. During the evening of lasciviousness naked local girls danced around to arouse sexual desire. The dissolution of the Order occurred on 30 November 1836.

A Chapter of the Order, known as the Wig Club, was founded in the 1760s at Edinburgh. The Chapter took its name from a Benison Club relic of a wig made from the pubic hair of the mistresses of Charles II, which had been originally given by Charles to the Earl of Moray. It was into this Club that George IV (then Prince of Wales) was given honorary membership at the suggestion of Sir Walter Scott. As the late Alan Bold points out in his introduction to the reprint of the 1892 edition of the Records of the Club: 'Apparently George IV suggested that the knights fashion a new wig and, as a right royal gesture, presented them with a silver snuffbox containing the pubic hair of his mistress.'

How did Buckingham Palace become the prime royal residence?

'Everything is so straggly, such distances and so fatiguing.'

– *Queen Victoria*.

'A sepulchre.' – *King Edward VII*.

'It has a dank and musty smell.' – *King Edward VIII*.

'An icebox.' – *King George VI*.

Monarchs' opinions of Buckingham Palace.

Buckingham Palace, with its address of Pimlico, London SW1, was originally the town house of the dukes of Buckingham. The palace was constructed during 1702–05 by William Winde for John Sheffield, 1st Duke of Buckingham and Normanby (1648–1721), who was given a parcel of land at the western end of St James's Park to add to his Buckingham House estate. It was rumoured that Queen Anne admired him as he had made advances towards her in 1682 when she was Princess Anne and was banished from court for his pains. The gift of land was a token of her remembrance.

In earlier days James I/VI had used the land for the cultivation of black mulberry trees. At the time the English aristocracy were much taken with the idea of making vast fortunes out of silk making; it was noted that the prime step towards such a fortune was to plant groves of mulberry trees in which the silk worms could breed. Alas for King James, it was *white* mulberry trees that nurtured silk worms. Thus the royal experiment failed. But the plot he set out became known as the Mulberry Garden and was a popular rendezvous for young lovers. Today a mulberry tree is still extant in the gardens of Buckingham Palace.

By 1633 George Goring, Earl of Norwich paid Charles I £400 for the rights to the Mulberry Garden and built himself a mansion known as Goring House. Alas in 1674 it was gutted by fire destroying the new owner, Henry Bennet, Earl of Arlington's fabulous antiques collection. Arlington, who is remembered in history as a procurer of pretty girls for Charles II, rebuilt Goring House as Arlington House and by purchase of land from Sir Thomas Grosvenor, expanded the estate. Thus the house and estate was sold by Arlington's daughter, the Duchess of Grafton, to John Sheffield.

Sheffield developed Buckingham House out of the property he had bought and it remained within the same family until it was bought for £21,000 in 1762 by George III. For a time it was known as Queen's House, the residence of George III's wife Queen Charlotte. The king spent £47,506 on alterations to the house which now resembled a country gentleman's property. The house became a focal point for Londoners to promenade and gossip outside its railings in the hope of catching a glimpse of the Royal Family. Here, too, in the Royal Mews was housed the State Coach purchased by George III in 1762 for £7,567 19s 9½d (£7,587.95); the coach is still in use today for state occasions. George III collected a fine library of books at Queen's House, which was to form the nucleus of the British Library. The first marriage to be conducted at the house was that of Frederick, Duke of York, George and Charlotte's second child, who married in 1791 Princess Frederica, eldest daughter of Frederick William II of Prussia.

When George IV succeeded to the throne in 1820 he decided to make the Queen's House his principle London residence and persuaded parliament to vote £252,690 for its repair. In the event George spent three times as much on its reconstruction and died before the palace was completed to the design of John Nash. George's successor and brother, Prince William, Duke of Clarence (later King William IV) was born at Buckingham Palace in 1765; the first royal to be born here. He hated the place, but finished off the work his brother had started to include gas lighting. Proving to be an open drain for cash Buckingham Palace was ready for occupation in May 1837. William IV died the following month. Queen Victoria inherited the palace and all but one of her children were born there, including Edward VII who was the only monarch to die at the palace. Final alterations to the palace were made in 1913 by the addition of the west front of Portland Stone to the design of Sir Aston Webb.

There are some 600 rooms in the palace including those used by the staff as offices and domestic quarters. The rooms privately occupied by the Royal Family are few in number. The queen and the Duke of Edinburgh have a suite of about a dozen rooms on the first floor of the north wing overlooking Green Park. The gardens of the palace, landscaped by W.T. Aiton, run to some 45 acres and extend to Hyde Park Corner.

Rumour and Scandal

Which monarch topped the list for siring royal bastards?

[The Duke of Clarence had] spread the falsest and most unnatural coloured pretence that man might imagine, that the King our most sovereign lord was a bastard, and not begotten to reign upon us.

Indictment against George, Duke of Clarence for slandering
his brother King Edward IV (1478).

Royal illegitimacy has been the stuff of 'skeletons in the royal cupboard' for generations, with people popping up all over the place to be 'royal bastards'. In 1981 the *Miami Herald* noted the death of Irene Victoria Alexandra Louise Isabel Bush. Her claim to royal ancestry was her assertion that she had been born in Ireland at Carton, County Kildare on 28 February 1899, as Lady Irene Fitzgerald Coburg, the daughter of one Mabel Fitzgerald and HRH Prince Alfred of Edinburgh and Saxe-Coburg

(1874–99), the son of Queen Victoria's second son Prince Alfred ('Affie'), 5th Duke of Edinburgh and Saxe Coburg, and his wife Marie Alexandrovna, Grand Duchess of Russia. Young Alfred was destined to the Duchy of Saxe-Coburg and was given 'a thorough German education'. During his service in the 1st Regiment of Prussia Guards he had led a dissipated life, which was a kind of solace for his troubled childhood and youth wherein he had endured 'a frequently absent father', an 'unsympathetic mother' and a martinet of a German tutor in Dr Wilhelm Rolfs. Around 1899 it appears that Alfred had married Mabel Fitzgerald, an Irish commoner, totally against the Royal Marriage Act of 1772. In 1899 Alfred, in a bout of severe depression, and suffering from venereal disease, shot himself at Meran in the Austrian Tyrol. However, he lasted a few days to die at Schloss Rosenau, Coburg on 10 February 1899. For decades Prince Alfred's demise was glossed over, as was his liaison with Mabel Fitzgerald and his putative daughter. Then in 1924 Walburga, Lady Paget, wrote of Prince Alfred's attempted suicide in her memoir *In My Tower* giving the lie that he had died of 'phthisis' (tuberculosis). His father's biographers John Van der Kiste and Bee Jordaan noted in 1984, 'The Royal Archives at Windsor … have intimated that the facts do not apply [sic]'.

Still assertions go on. In 2006 a Jersey accountant, Robert Brown, made the bizarre claim that he was the illegitimate nephew of Queen Elizabeth II, being the 'love child' of the late Princess Margaret, Countess of Snowdon. Brown averred that he was born in 1955 following an affair between Princess Margaret and the man she was once in love with, Group Captain Peter Townsend or, said Brown, from her well-publicised affair with the late Robin Douglas-Home. His claim received only publicity in the press.

Royal illegitimacy is a matter of state record since at least the eleventh century, with William the Conqueror – William the Bastard – the illegitimate son of Robert I of Normandy by Herleve, a girl from Falaise where Robert had a castle, being one of the most famous royal illegitimates in history. Yet what do royal records show about other royal bastards?

HOUSE OF NORMANDY

HENRY I (r. 1100–35):

Purported to have twenty-five illegitimate children by six known women and others unknown. Four children paternity uncertain.

He had six children by Sybilla Corbet of Alcester:

❖ Robert, Earl of Gloucester, married Mabel Fitzhamon. Issue. d. 1147.

❖ Reginald, Earl of Cornwall, married Beatrice Fitzrichard. Issue. d. 1175.

❖ William, married Alice. Issue not known. d. *c.* 1187.

❖ Sybilla, married Alexander I, King of Scots. No issue. d. 1122.

❖ Gundrada. Background not known.

❖ Rohese married Henry de la Pomerai. Issue. d. *c.* 1176.

He had three children by Ansfrida widow of Anskill, a knight:

❖ Richard of Lincoln. Died on 25 November 1120 in the White Ship disaster.

❖ Brother Fulk, a monk. (Name of several Counts of Anjou.)

❖ Juliana, married Eustace de Pacy, Lord of Bréteuil. Issue. d. 1136, a nun.

By Nest, daughter of Rhys ap Tewdwr, King of Deheubarth, SW Wales, one son:

❖ Henry Fitzhenry. Issue. d. 1157 in battle.

By Edith Sigulfson of Greystoke, one son:

❖ Robert Fitzedith, Baron of Okehampton, married Maud d'Avranches. Issue. d. 1172.

By Isabel de Beaumont, daughter of the Earl of Leicester, two daughters:

❖ Isabella who died unmarried *c.* 1120, and Matilda, Abbess of Montivilliers.

By Edith, one daughter:

❖ Matilda, who died in the White Ship disaster. She married Rotrou II, Count of Perche. Issue.

STEPHEN (r. 1135–54):

At least five illegitimates, including Gervase, Abbot of Westminster.

Children by mothers unknown:

❖ Gilbert. d. *c.* 1142.
❖ William de Tracy. Issue. d. *c.* 1136.
❖ Matilda, married Conan II, Duke of Brittany. Issue.
❖ Constance, married Roscelin de Beaumont. Issue; a granddaughter, Ermengarde, married William I, The Lion, King of Scots and had four children, including King Alexander II.
❖ Eustacia, married William Gouet III, Lord of Montmireil. Issue.
❖ Alice, married Mathew de Montmorenci, Constable of France. Issue.

(There is a record that an unknown daughter was betrothed to William de Warenne; but never married.)

Records show four more children of uncertain paternity:

❖ Joan, married Fergus of Galloway. Issue.

❖ Emma, married Guy de Laval. Issue.

❖ Sybilla, married Baldwin de Boullers.

(Records show an unknown daughter betrothed to Hugh Fitzgervais; never married.)

HOUSE OF ANJOU

HENRY II (r. 1154–89):

He had twelve illegitimates by five or more mothers.

❖ Geoffrey Plantagenet, Bishop-elect of Lincoln (1173), Royal Chancellor.

❖ William Longsword.

RICHARD I (r. 1189–99):

Possibly two illegitimates.

JOHN (r. 1199–1216):

He had at least twelve illegitimates. These included:

❖ Geoffrey.

❖ Joan, married Llewelyn ap Ioworth, mother Clementina.

❖ Oliver.

❖ Richard.

❖ Osbert.

EDWARD I (r. 1272–1307):

He had one disputed illegitimate.

EDWARD II (r. 1307–27):

He had one known illegitimate, Adam.

EDWARD III (r. 1327–77):

He had possibly three illegitimates by his mistress Alice Perrers (*c.* 1348–1400), maid of Queen Philippa's Bedchamber. Jane and Joan are known names.

HOUSE OF YORK

EDWARD IV (r. 1461–70):

He had two known illegitimates.

❖ Arthur Plantagenet, Viscount Lisle by Elizabeth Lucy, and one daughter of whom little is known.

RICHARD III (r. 1483–85):

He had four known illegitimates of which two are prominent:

❖ John of Gloucester, titular Captain of Calais. No issue.
❖ Katherine Plantagenet, married in 1484 to the Earl of Huntingdon. No issue.

HOUSE OF TUDOR

HENRY VII (r. 1485–1509):

He had one disputed illegitimate.

HENRY VIII (r. 1509–47):

He had two recorded illegitimates.

During the festivities of New Year 1514, Henry's eye was caught by one of Queen Catherine of Aragon's ladies-in-waiting, Elizabeth 'Bessie' Blount, cousin of William Blount, 4th Baron Mountjoy. She became Henry's 'official' mistress and bore him a son in June 1519, Henry Fitzroy, Duke of Richmond and Somerset (so created in 1525), Earl of Nottingham, Lord High Admiral, Lt Gen North of the Trent, Warden of All the Marches up to Scotland. When it was clear that Catherine of Aragon was incapable of bearing King Henry a son it is thought that he had a mind to make Henry Fitzroy his legitimate heir and talked of making him King of Ireland. This came to naught. Bessie Blount was 'packed off to the country' in 1522 with one of Cardinal Wolsey's protégé's Gilbert Tallboys; Henry gave the young couple the Manor of Rokeby to live their lives henceforth in obscurity.

Although it was once proposed that Henry Fitzroy marry his half-sister Princess Mary Tudor (even though this was against canon law) he married Mary Howard, daughter of the Duke of Norfolk, sister of his childhood playmate Henry Howard, Earl of Surrey. Henry Fitzroy died in 1536; rumour had it that he was poisoned by King Henry's second wife Anne Boleyn, but modern historians log his demise as being from tuberculosis; he was childless. Mary died in 1557.

HOUSE OF STUART

CHARLES II (r. 1650–85):
He had sixteen illegitimates by eight mistresses.

By Lucy Walter of Haverfordwest (*c.* 1630–58):
❖ James, Duke of Monmouth, married Anne Scott of Buccleuch (1651–1732). Issue. d. 1685.

By Elizabeth Killigrew, later Lady Shannon:
❖ Charlotte Fitzroy, married William, Earl of Yarmouth. Issue. d. 1684.

By Barbara Villiers (1641–1709), later Duchess of Cleveland:

- ❖ Anne Fitzroy, married Henry Lennard, Earl of Sussex. No issue. d. 1722.
- ❖ Charles Fitzroy, Duke of Southampton and Cleveland, married (2) Anne Poultney (1663–1745). Issue. d. 1730.
- ❖ Henry Fitzroy, Duke of Grafton, married Isabella Bennett (d. 1723). Issue. d. 1690.
- ❖ George Fitzroy, Duke of Northumberland, twice married. No issue. d. 1716.
- ❖ Barbara Benedicte, Prioress. Some historians suggest that she was the daughter of John Churchill, Duke of Marlborough.

By Nell Gwynne (1650–87):

- ❖ Charles Beauclerk, Duke of St Albans, married Diane de Vere (d. 1742). Issue. d. 1726.
- ❖ James Beauclerk. d. 1680.

By Louise de Kéroüaille (1649–1734), Duchess of Portsmouth:

- ❖ Charles Lennox, Duke of Richmond and Duke of Aubigny, married Anne Brudenell. Issue. d. 1723.
- ❖ Mary 'Moll' Davies.
- ❖ Mary Tudor. d. 1726. Mary was married three times, but by her second and third husbands, Henry Graham of Levens and James Rooke, respectively, she had no children. By her first husband, Edward, Earl of Derwentwater (d.1705), she had children who became significant in Jacobite history. James (1689–1716) was executed for his part in the Jacobite rebellion of 1715; Charles (1693–1746) became private secretary to Prince Charles Edward Stuart and was executed for his part in the Jacobite rebellion of 1745.

The current dukes of Buccleuch and Queensberry, Grafton, St Albans, Richmond and Gordon are all direct descendants of Charles II's illegitimate children. Other connections can be made through the convolutions of family tree branches. For instance, Ralph George Algenon Percy, 12th Duke of Northumberland (b. 1956), although nothing to do with the title created for Barbara Villiers's second son, is related to Charles II and Louise de Kéroüalle, and to Charles II and Lucy Walter as his mother was a daughter of the 8th Duke of Buccleuch and his grandmother a daughter of the 7th Duke of Richmond.

JAMES II/VII (r .1685–88):

He had seven illegitimates by two mothers.

One significant offspring of four was by Arabella Churchill (1648–1730), maid in waiting to Queen Anne Hyde, sister of John Churchill, Duke of Marlborough:

❖ James Fitzjames, Duke of Berwick, Marshal of France.
   d. 1734.

HOUSE OF HANOVER

GEORGE I (r. 1714–27):

He had three illegitimates by his German *maîtress en titre* the 'tall and lean of stature' Ehrengard Melusina von der Schulenberg (1667–1747), Duchess of Kendal, nicknamed 'The Maypole'. (There were persistent rumours that George had married her 'with his left hand' according to the Continental custom of kings marrying commoners.)

GEORGE II (r. 1727–60):
He had one recorded illegitimate.

GEORGE IV (r. 1820–30):
He had some six possible illegitimates, including Lord Albert, by his mistress Elizabeth, Marchioness of Conyngham, and of which three are considered 'most certain'.

By Grace Eliot:
❖ Georgina Augusta Frederica Seymour, b. 30 March 1782, married Lord Charles Bentinck, 1808.

By Elizabeth Fox (Mrs Crole):
❖ George, b. 23 August 1799, followed a privileged military career.

By Lucy Howard:
❖ George Howard (*c.* 1818–20).

WILLIAM IV (r. 1830–37):
He had ten illegitimates with his mistress, comedy actress Dorothy Jordan (Bland), (1761–1816):

❖ George Augustus Frederick Fitzclarence, 1st Earl of Munster, b. 29 January 1794. Married Mary Wyndham Fox, daughter of the Earl of Egremont. Committed suicide, 20 March 1842.
❖ Sophia Fitzclarence, b. 4 March 1795. Married Philip, 1st Baron De L'Isle and Dudley. d. 10 April 1837 in childbirth.
❖ Henry Edward Fitzclarence, b. 8 March 1797. d. 3 September 1817.

- ❖ Mary Fitzclarence, b. 19 December 1798. Married Charles Fox, illegitimate son of Henry, Baron Holland and Elizabeth Vassall. d. 13 July 1864.
- ❖ Frederick Fitzclarence, b. 9 December 1799. Married Lady Augusta Boyle, daughter of George, Earl of Glasgow. d. 30 October 1854.
- ❖ Elizabeth Fitzclarence, b. 17 January 1801. Married William Hay, Earl of Erroll, 16 January 1856. Their daughter Lady Agnes was mother-in-law to Louise, Princess Royal, eldest daughter of Edward VII.
- ❖ Adolphus Fitzclarence, b. 17 February 1802. d. 17 May 1856, unmarried.
- ❖ Augusta Fitzclarence, b. 17 November 1803. Married (1) John Kennedy-Erskine of Dun, second son of the 1st Marquis of Alisa (d. 1831); (2) Lord Frederick Gordon, son of the 9th Marquis of Huntly. (d. 1878). Issue by first marriage. d. 8 December 1865.
- ❖ Revd Augustus Fitzclarence, b. 1 March 1805. Married Sarah Elizabeth Gordon, eldest daughter of Lord Henry Gordon, fourth son of the Marquis of Huntly. Rector of Mapledurham, Oxfordshire. d. 14 June 1854.
- ❖ Amelia Fitzclarence, b. 21 March 1807. Married Lucius Bentinck Cary, 10th Viscount Falkland. d. 2 July 1858.

So by extant records Henry I, with twenty-five purported illegitimates, tops the list of siring royal bastards. But what of the monarchs of Scotland?

WILLIAM I, THE LION (r. 1165–1214):
He had nine purported illegitimates.

ALEXANDER II (r. 1214–49):
He had one illegitimate daughter.

ROBERT II (r. 1371–98):
He had at least eight illegitimates.

ROBERT III (r. 1390–1406):
He had one illegitimate child.

JAMES II (r. 1437–60):
He had one illegitimate child.

JAMES IV (r. 1488–1513):
He had at least seven illegitimates. His most prominent were:

By Mariot Boyd, daughter of Archibald Boyd, Laird of Bonshaw:
- ❖ Alexander Stewart, b. 1493. Archdeacon of St Andrews aged 9; Archbishop of St Andrews aged 11; Chancellor of the University of St Andrews, founder of St Leonard's College, 1512. Died with his father at the Battle of Flodden, 9 September 1513.
- ❖ Catherine, b. 1494.

By Janet Kennedy, daughter of John, Lord Kennedy:
- ❖ James Stewart, Earl of Moray, created 1501.

By Isabel Stuart, daughter of James, Earl of Buchan, a child, details unknown.

JAMES V (r. 1513–42):
He had at least nine illegitimates, of which the most prominent in history was by Margaret Erskine, wife of Robert Douglas of Lochleven:

❖ James Stewart, Earl of Moray. b.1531. Commendator of St Andrews Priory aged 7. He became the chief minister of his half-sister Mary, Queen of Scots, thereafter Regent of Scotland on her abdication. He was murdered by James Hamilton of Bothwellhaugh at Linlithgow on 23 January 1570.

Which British monarchs were put in prison or appeared in court?

King Henry VI was a very ignorant and almost simple man and, unless I have been deceived, immediately after the battle the Duke of Gloucester, Edward's brother, who later became King Richard killed this good man with his own hand or at least had him killed in his presence in some obscure place.

Philippe de Commynes, Memoirs *(c. 1498).*

Like Henry VI who ended his life at the Tower of London, many of royal birth have spent years in prison, quite often because they were in the way of others who wished to succeed to the throne. One such was Edward Plantagenet, nephew of Edward IV and Richard III. He was imprisoned both by Richard III and Henry VII. In prison since childhood, Edward was executed on a 'trumped-up charge' of treason in November 1499; he had been in prison for fifteen and a half years. In Scotland David, Duke of Rothesay (b.1378), heir apparent to Robert III, was imprisoned at Falkland Castle in 1402 on the urgings of his uncle the Duke of Albany and his father-in-law the Earl of Douglas, to die in obscure circumstances a few months later.

Undoubtedly the most romantic prisoner was Mary, Queen of Scots, who spent nineteen years, seven months and ten days as a prisoner of Queen Elizabeth I, until her execution at Fotheringay on 8 February 1587. Again, two royal prisoners whose story is steeped in mystery and pity are the 12-year-old Edward V and his 9-year-old brother Richard, Duke of York, the famous 'Princes in the Tower' who 'disappeared' some time after 1483. Charles I also suffered trial and imprisonment. He surrendered to the Scots about a year after the Battle of Naseby on 14 July 1645, to be imprisoned at Newcastle and Hampton Court (from which he escaped) and Carisbrooke Castle. In January 1649 he was brought to trial for treason at a court he did not recognise as legal; he was found guilty of the charge that he had fought against his subjects and was executed at Whitehall Palace, 30 January 1649.

Queen Consorts fared little better. For thirty-nine years Eleanor of Brittany, niece of kings Richard I and John, was imprisoned because of her superior claims to rule England over King John. She died at Bristol Castle, 10 August 1241. Isabella of France, daughter of Philippe IV of France, queen of Edward II, was imprisoned for just over twenty-eight years. With her lover Roger Mortimer, she plotted the overthrowal and death of Edward II. Her imprisonment at Castle Rising, Norfolk, lasted from April 1330 until her death on 22 August 1358. Other kings died in incarceration. Edward II was murdered at Berkley Castle, Gloucestershire, on 21 September 1327; and Richard II was starved to death at Pontefract Castle to die around 14 February 1400.

Three Scottish kings stand out as royal prisoners. Duncan II (d.1094), son of Malcolm III and his first wife, Ingibjord, were taken as hostages by William I, the Conqueror, during one of his father's five fruitless raids into Norman suzerainty in England. Historians believe that Malcolm favoured as his heirs his children by his second wife Margaret, granddaughter of Edmund II of England, with possible disinheritance. Duncan spent fifteen years in Norman captivity. Duncan was killed in battle in 1094 after his invasion of Scotland to win his throne from Donald III who had usurped it on Malcolm's death in 1093.

David II (r.1329–32; 1332–33; 1336–71), son of Robert I, the Bruce, and Elizabeth de Burgh, was taken prisoner after he had invaded England at the Battle of Neville's Cross, near Durham, on 17 October 1346. He was released under the terms of the Treaty of Berwick of October 1357 for a ransom of 100,000 marks, of which the balance was never paid. David was thus in what has been described as 'agreeable captivity' in London and Hampshire for just under eleven years.

James I (r.1406–37), son of Robert III and Annabella Drummond, tops the list of royal prisoners who were held in custody while still reigning. At the age of 11 James was captured at sea while on his way to safety in France from lawless Scotland. He was handed over by pirates to Henry IV to be confined first at the Tower of London and then Nottingham Castle. He was allowed to vacillate at the English court, and eventually married in 1424 Lady Joan Beaufort, great-granddaughter of Edward III; this was the year of his coronation in Scotland, his release coming after the death of Henry IV in 1422. James was assassinated at Perth, 21 February 1437. In all, James had been in confinement for almost eighteen years.

A number of British royals appeared in law courts for various reasons, from Cardinal Wolsey's opening of the 'Secret Trial of the King's Marriage' on 17 May 1527, concerning Henry's divorce of Queen Catherine of Aragon, to the proceedings against Queen Caroline, wife of George IV during August–November 1820, when she appeared in the House of Lords on charges of immorality. Only one subsequent British monarch appeared in a civil court.

As Prince of Wales, Edward VII appeared in court as a witness, twice. In 1890 he was called to the civil court in what is known to historians as the 'Royal Baccarat Scandal' but twenty years earlier he appeared in more serious circumstances, for since the reign of Henry IV no Prince of Wales had ever stood before a Court of Justice.

Albert Edward, Prince of Wales, was drawn into the 'Mordaunt Case' because of his vigorous and hectic social life. Lady Harriet Mordaunt (d.1906), one of the daughters of Sir Thomas Moncrieffe, was an attractive 21 year old who appeared regularly at Edward's parties from Abergeldie near Balmoral to Marlborough House, London. Her husband, Sir Charles Mordaunt (1836–97), was Tory MP for South Warwickshire and was many years her senior. To all in society Harriet appeared 'excitable and highly strung'. Following the birth of her first child, Violet (later Marchioness of Bath), in 1869, the premature infant was diagnosed with what Harriet interpreted as threatened blindness. This she told people was caused by a 'fearful disease' (i.e. venereal contagion). As time passed Harriet exhibited postpartum depression leading to increased eccentricity of behaviour. She told her husband that the child was not his and that she had committed adultery 'often and in open day' with Lowry Egerton, Lord Cole, Sir Frederick Johnstone and the Prince of Wales among others. She identified Lord Cole as the father of Violet. Instead of dismissing the confession as nonsense, Mordaunt chose to believe his wife. The child was soon cured of a mild eye infection and there were no traces of venereal infection in either Harriet or her infant.

Incensed by her confession Mordaunt forced open her private desk and removed a diary and correspondence Harriet had had with the Prince of Wales and others. Although Edward had sent her a valentine card as well, the eleven extant letters from him were innocuous social gossip, but Mordaunt filed for divorce. Edward strongly voiced his innocence, the Lord Chancellor, Lord Hatherley, pronounced the letters to Harriet as 'unexceptional in every way', and the Lord Chief Justice, Sir Alexander Cockburn, advised Edward of what would happen in court. Yes, Edward had written to Harriet; yes, he had visited her on several occasions; but, no, he had not had sexual intimacy with her. Alexandra, Princess of Wales, believed her husband and publicly supported him. When the facts were communicated to an aghast Queen Victoria she telegraphed her support for her son, adding that he should be more circumspect in future when dealing with young married women. The anti-royal press, like the *Reynolds's Newspaper*, had a field day stirring up wide public interest in the trial, which was heard before Lord Penzance in the Court for Divorce and Matrimonial Causes in Westminster Hall, and before a special jury on 23 February 1870 (postponed from the 16th).

Edward was not cited as a co-respondent, a counter-petition having been filed by Sir Thomas Moncrieffe on his daughter's behalf to the effect that Harriet was clinically insane; at that time she was already in an asylum. Edward was only subpoenaed by Harriet's counsel Dr Francis Deane as a witness. The prince, who had shown great nervousness at the thought of appearing in court, was confident in the witness box. It appears that Sir Charles Mordaunt had suspected his wife of illicit liaisons for some time but had kept quiet. Yet, on returning home to Walton Hall (his country house in Warwickshire) he found Harriet showing off her driving skills to the Prince of Wales. When Edward had gone Sir Charles had the ponies he had given to her shot before her eyes. The testimony further heard by the jury shed public light on Edward's social habits of visiting attractive married women when their husbands were out. They heard from Mordaunt's butler and a ladies' maid how the prince had visited Harriet in 1867 and 1868 several times. The butler said: 'Lady Mordaunt gave me directions that when the Prince called no one was to be admitted.' Occasionally Edward would arrive in a hansom cab. Then came the blunt question from Mordaunt's counsel, Mr Serjeant Thomas Ballantyne: 'Has there ever been any improper familiarity or criminal act between yourself and Lady Mordaunt?'

'There has not,' replied the prince, to much applause from spectators in the public gallery (admonished by Lord Penzance). There was no cross-examination and Edward's 'ordeal' only lasted seven minutes. Sir Charles Mordaunt's petition for divorce was dismissed on the grounds that Harriet Mordaunt was clearly insane and 'could not be a party to the suit'. Much litigation followed the case, yet on 11 March 1875, Mordaunt was granted his divorce. Before setting off to dine with Prime Minister W.E. Gladstone, that night the Prince of Wales wrote this to Queen Victoria:

> I trust by what I have said today that the public at large will be satisfied that the gross imputations which have been so wantonly cast upon me are now cleared up.

The Prince of Wales had not been on trial, but the public found him guilty. *Reynolds's Newspaper* voiced the widespread public disapproval of the Prince of Wales's conduct and hoped that Queen Victoria's health would be robust to defer the Prince of Wales's accession to the throne; within days of the trial he was publicly booed at the theatre and at Epsom races. Queen Victoria said she believed that the Prince of Wales's conduct in public did 'damage him in the eyes of the middle and lower classes' and that he should spend less time in the company of the 'frivolous, selfish and pleasure-seeking rich'. The Prince of Wales ignored her.

Was there a case of incest in the Royal Family?

... a very delicate subject [arises] – the cruelty of a fabricated and most scandalous and base report concerning P.S. [Princess Sophia].

Letter of March 1801 from Princess Elizabeth to Dr Thomas Willis.

Princess Sophia was born at Queen's House, Kensington, on 3 November 1777, the fifth daughter and eleventh child (of fifteen) of George III and Queen Charlotte. Beloved of her siblings, Sophia never married; she died in 1848 blind like her father and, according to the backbiting of the time, she had an illegitimate baby. By the 'cackle of gossip' and the 'savagery of politics', the affair was reinvented as an incestuous illegitimacy with her brother Prince Ernest, Duke of Cumberland, later King of Hanover.

Never of robust health Sophia was kept mainly at Windsor along with her sisters, in a close confinement by the orders and presence of Queen Charlotte. Sophia was seriously ill at Weymouth during January–October 1800, to be attended by Physician to the Royal Household (later Sir) Francis Milman. According to his records the princess was suffering from 'spasms', but somehow gossip was developed that the 'spasms' were actually a cover-up for pregnancy. By the end of 1800 it is clear that Sophia knew what was being said about her. She wrote this to Elizabeth, Countess Harcourt: 'It is grievous to think what a little trifle will slur a young woman's character for ever.' Could she really have considered pregnancy 'a little trifle', later historians wondered?

Who initiated the pregnancy story? Historians believe that it was 'fostered' and 'embellished ... with its malignant horror' by Princess Caroline of Brunswick (1768–1821), wife of Sophia's brother George, Prince of Wales. Caroline was a poisonous member of the Royal Family, who constantly sought revenge for the 'humiliation of her marriage' (George parted from Caroline for ever after the birth of their daughter in 1796). Caroline's gossiping concerned many of the Royal Family, from George III who she said had 'freedoms with her of the grossest nature' to anecdotes about changeling infants and incestuous relationships. All were laughed off by family and courtiers alike. But why did the gossip about Princess Sophia remain for generations?

Writing in 1977 in *Society Scandals* the historian Sir Roger Thomas Baldwin Fulford (1902–83), set out a theory of how Princess Sophia was so accused. He identifies the lawyer-turned-politician Sylvester Douglas, Lord Glenbervie (1743–1823) as a diarist who married the elder daughter of Prime Minister Lord North. She was lady-in-waiting to the Princess of Wales and, through her, titbits of gossip about Princess Sophia appeared in his diary. Glenbervie wrote on 25 March 1801:

> I heard yesterday a recapitulation of many of the circumstances of the Princess Sophia's extraordinary illness last autumn at Weymouth ... They are too delicate a nature for me to commit them ... even to this safe repository. But they are such as leave scarce a doubt in my mind.

He later noted that the 'extraordinary illness' was a pregnancy and that the child's father was General Thomas Garth (1774–1829), equerry to George III. Glenbervie went on to say that 'the Weymouth foundling' was christened Thomas and was lodged at the house in Weymouth of Col Herbert Taylor, George III's private secretary. Garth was a long-trusted friend of the Royal Family and a prominent courtier. Fulford dismisses Glenbervie's accusations with: 'would they [the princess's siblings] have allowed one who had behaved in this way to their favourite sister to remain in the Court circle?' Fulford further quotes the diarist Charles Greville who said of Garth: 'he is a hideous old Devil, old enough to be [Sophia's] father, and with a great claret mark on his face.'

Thus Fulford dismisses Garth as being an improbable lover and says that the 'scandalmongers' were made to 'dig deeper'. So he identifies Glenbervie as saying: 'the Duke of Kent [Prince Edward] tells the Princess [of Wales] that the father is not Garth but the Duke of Cumberland. How horrid!' A womanising blackguard,

Cumberland was a popular target for invective and the incest story would have had willing listeners who believed, as Christopher Hibbert put it, that '[Cumberland's] watchful affection for [Sophia] was certainly felt to be unnatural'. Fulford dismisses the stories of Princess Sophia's pregnancy and quotes Henry Petty-Fitzmaurice, Marquis of Landsdowne on Princess Sophia's death: 'Her Royal Highness has passed a long life of virtue, charity and excellence in every position, public and private, in which she was placed.' Other historians have had a different opinion.

In 1882 Percy Fitzgerald noted that 'there was a secret morganatic marriage between General Garth and Sophia', and others, like Anthony Bird, attested that she gave birth to the offspring Thomas Garth Jr who was 'a thoroughly unpleasant and unprincipled young man'. Fitzgerald went on: 'there seems to have been no doubt in the [Royal] Family about his parentage.' During one illness, which was deemed terminal, General Garth entrusted to his son 'very incriminating papers' about the illegitimacy. Garth Jr promptly attempted to blackmail the Royal Family.

In her reassessment of the six daughters of George III in 2004, Flora Fraser added that a child (purporting to be Sophia's) was baptised at Weymouth on 11 August 1800. Born on 5 August the child, 'Thomas Ward, stranger' (or foundling) was 'adopted by Samuel and Charlotte Sharland'. Was this child's entry a royal cover-up? We shall probably never know, but the charge of incest against Cumberland is summed up by his biographer Anthony Bird:

> The canard that Cumberland added incest to his crimes became accepted as an article of faith and is believed to this day [1966] – for the vilification of his character continues.

Did Edward VII have a 'secret family'?

> If you were to try and deny it [that Edward had fathered an illegitimate child], she [Nellie Clifton] can drag you into a court of law to force you to own it & there with you in the witness box, she will be able to give before a greedy Multitude disgusting details of your profligacy for the sake of convincing the Jury; yourself crossexamined by a railing indecent attorney and hooted and yelled at by a Lawless Mob!! Oh horrible prospect, which this person has in her power, any day to realise! and to break your poor parents' hearts!
>
> *Albert Consort, to Edward, Prince of Wales on discovering that Edward had had sexual relations with Nellie Cliften while on military service at The Curragh, Ireland.*

When King Edward VII breathed his last at 11.45 p.m. on 6 May 1910 at Buckingham Palace, surrounded by Queen Alexandra, George and Mary, the Prince and Princess of Wales, Louise, the Princess Royal, Duchess of Fife, daughter of Princess Victoria and sister Princess Louise, Duchess of Argyll, the international press rushed into print with eulogies on Edward as the 'Uncle of Europe' and his devoted family. None mentioned his 'secret family' of supposed children, products of decades of philandering in and out of the boudoirs of some of society's beauties.

Leonie Blanche Jerome (1859–1943), wife of Col (later Sir) John Leslie (1857–1944) and sister of Jennie, Lady Randolph Churchill, had in her possession at Castle Leslie, Co. Monaghan, Ireland a photo album, one of its pages containing an intriguing picture. It showed the image of one Baroness de Meyer and, said writer Anita Leslie, 'lightly pencilled under the name [was the caption] "daughter of Edward VII"'.

The Baroness was the daughter of Blanche, Duchesse de Caracciolo, who seems to have separated from her husband on her wedding day to return for a while to her philandering lover, Prince Josef Poniatowski, a current equerry to Emperor Napoleon III. During the late 1860s, Edward, Prince of Wales, met her and when she fell pregnant around 1868 arranged for her to live with his supposed baby daughter, Alberta Olga Caracciolo, at a cliff-top villa at Dieppe, where he visited her when passing in a borrowed yacht. The house became the Villa Olga and was dubbed *La Villa Mystère* by locals, and Edward's visits were well known among the resident English elite. Lee Jortin, the local English consul, monitored Edward's visits. Blanche later recalled: 'When the august parent of [Alberta] Olga came incognito we were supposed not to know, although plain-clothes policemen paraded our quarter in relays day and night.' Edward stood godfather to baby Alberta Olga. In later life the pretty girl would be drawn and painted by Sickert, Whistler, Boldini, Helleu and Jacques-Emile Blanche in 1887. In due course Alberta Olga married the society photographer Adolphe de Meyer and Edward prevailed upon Albert, the Wettin King of Saxony to confer a Saxon barony on de Meyer so that Alberta Olga could attend his coronation in 1902 as a baroness. The de Meyers were regular guests of members of the louche (the Prince of Wales's) circle, for instance enjoying the after Ascot week with the Ernest Becketts, he who fathered Edward's mistress the Hon. Mrs George Keppel's daughter Violet.

In September 1871 the Prince of Wales received a letter while at Abergeldie containing these words: 'Without any funds to meet the necessary expenses and to buy the discretion of servants, it is impossible to keep this sad secret.' The letter had come from a Mrs Harriet Whatman, a friend of his mistress since 1867 Lady Susan Pelham-Clinton, and announced the impending birth of his child. Lady Susan Charlotte Catherine was the daughter of Henry

Pelham-Clinton, 5th Duke of Newcastle, a mentor to the Prince of Wales and a great friend of Queen Victoria and Prince Albert; Lady Susan had been a bridesmaid to the Princess Royal in 1858. On 23 April 1860 she married against parental wishes the clinically insane Lt Col Adolphus Vane-Tempest (b. 1825), third son of Charles Stewart, 3rd Marquis of Londonderry. He died in 1864 having had some kind of 'struggle' with his keepers.

Edward was annoyed that Lady Susan had not informed him concerning the pregnancy. She said that she had done so to protect one she 'loved and honoured', and she had contemplated an abortion. Only when her financial situation worsened did she contact Edward, who she had not seen for some time. Through Edward's private secretary Francis Knollys, Lady Susan was given instructions to see Edward's 'confidential practitioner' Dr (later Sir) Oscar Clayton. But history does not show whether or not an abortion took place; certainly the fate of the child is not known. Lady Susan was still too ill in 1872 to attend the service of thanksgiving for the recovery of Edward from typhoid, although he sent her tickets. Lady Susan died on 6 September 1875, still in her thirties. Years later it was discovered that Edward had kept all of her love letters, enabling historians to add detail to the story of one of Edward's best attested illegitimate children.

Servants' gossip was always a good source of material for stories about the Prince of Wales being 'susceptible to feminine charms'. When the little daughter of an employee on the Eaton Hall estate in Cheshire of Hugh Grosvenor, 1st Duke of Westminster reported to her father that she had seen Edward 'lying on top of Mrs Cornwallis-West in the woods', she was hit with 'a violent blow and told she'd be killed if she repeated the story'. Mary 'Patsy' Cornwallis-West was born Mary Fitzpatrick in 1858 and when she was 17 she married Col William Cornwallis-West of the 1st Volunteer Battalion, Royal Welsh Guards and of Ruthin Castle, Wales. Patsy was the kind of woman the Prince of Wales liked; she was flirty, sexy and fun – her favourite party trick was to slide down the stairs on a tea-tray. In 1874 Patsy gave birth to George to whom Edward became godfather. In his autobiography *Edwardian Hey-Days* George wrote:

> The Prince of Wales often came [to the Cornwallis-West London home at No. 49 Eaton Square] and was invariably kind to me and always asked to see me. Never a Christmas passed without his sending me some little gift in the shape of a card or a toy.

In 1900 George married Jennie, Lady Randolph Churchill (against Edward's advice); they divorced in 1913. In all Patsy had three children to include Daisy and Constance. The Prince of Wales monitored George's career in the army, carefully using his influence when necessary.

It was widely believed that Edward was George's father. Writing in 2003, biographer Tim Coates said that Edward 'was a lover of many women and father of many children, including possibly all of Patsy's'. Patsy's two daughters also rose high in society. Daisy (d. 1943) married Prince Hans of Pless, and Constance (known as Shelagh, d. 1970) married Bendor, 2nd Duke of Westminster, and George married for a second time the actress Stella Patrick Campbell (d. 1940). Patsy Cornwallis-West died on 21 July 1920 at Arnewood, Near Newlands, in the New Forest.

The Prince of Wales was further rumoured to have fathered a child with the Princesse Jeanne-Marguerite Seillière de Sagan, wife of the Duc de Talleyrand-Périgord, whom he had first met during his visit to Louis Napoleon at Fontainebleau in 1862. Whenever he was in France Edward made efforts to meet her and visited her mostly at her home at the Château de Mello, south of Paris. There, a well-attested incident took place. Her eldest son, on being curious why his mother lunched alone in her boudoir with Edward, crept into the room to find the Prince of Wales's clothes spread over a chair. Gathering them up he threw them all out of the window to flutter down into a fountain in the gardens below. When Edward emerged from the princess's bedroom his sodden clothes were being fished out of the fountain. He had to return to Paris in borrowed clothes which did not fit him. It is said by French historians that the princess's second son, Prince Hélie de Sagan, was Edward's child. Aristocratic gossips further inferred that Chief Constable of Edinburgh Roderick Ross was also a child of Edward, as was Sir Stewart Graham Menzies, 'C' of the British Intelligence Service MI6.

In more recent times the art collector Edward James (1907–84) said that his mother, Evelyn 'Evie' Elizabeth James (1869–1930), was the illegitimate daughter of the Prince of Wales. She was officially the eldest daughter of Sir Charles Forbes, fourth baronet of Castle Newe, not far from Balmoral; her mother being Helen Moncrieff. Evie, noted James's biographer John Lowe, was 'the result of an indiscreet romp in the Highland heather between the young Prince of Wales and Helen …' It is said that the union was well known in aristocratic circles and Evie was a regular visitor to Balmoral as a child. Evie married William Dodge James who bought in 1891 West Dean Park, West Sussex, which became a place of royal visits. At West Dean Park a collection of royal letters was found on Evie's death which Edward James cited as proof of his mother's parentage.

Edward VII had six legitimate children with his wife Alexandra of Denmark and, considering Edward's life of serial adultery, perhaps several more from the wrong side of the blanket. Today there are still many in aristocratic families who believe that in their family trees are members of Edward's 'secret family'.

Were some of Queen Victoria's great-grandchildren supporters of Adolf Hitler's National Socialists?

I never thought Hitler was such a bad chap.

Prince Edward, Duke of Windsor, during an interview in 1970.
(Richard Woods, Sunday Times, 16 January 2005).

In a radio address from Windsor Castle on the evening of 11 December 1936, Edward VIII endeavoured to explain to the British Nation and Commonwealth why he had shocked them by abdicating his role as monarch. He said: 'I have found it impossible to carry the heavy burden of responsibility and to discharge my duties as King as I would wish to do without the help and support of the woman I love …' That woman was Mrs Wallis Warfield Simpson (1896–1986), the twice-divorced native of Baltimore, Maryland, and he was Edward Albert Christian George Andrew Patrick David (1894–1972), eldest son of George V and Queen Mary, and great-grandson of Queen Victoria. Edward and Wallis were married in the salon at the Château de Candé in the Loire Valley, France, on 3 June 1937 and lived the rest of their lives in exile as the Duke and Duchess of Windsor. Later that year the Duke and Duchess embarked on a visit that enraged sections of public opinion in Britain, caused the new King George VI to call it 'a bombshell and a bad one', and historians to ask: 'What was behind the Duke of Windsor's purported flirtation with Adolf Hitler?'

Despite such legislation as the promulgation of the racist Nuremberg laws of 1935 and the clear evidence that National Socialist Germany was rearming in violation of the Versailles Agreement of 1919, the Duke and Duchess of Windsor met the Führer of the Third German Reich, Adolf Hitler on 22 October 1937, at his mountaintop villa, the Berghof, above Berchtesgaden. While in Germany they met deputy leader and Reich Minister Rudolf Hess and the flamboyant Reichsmarschall Herman Göring.

Why were the Windsors there at all? The visit had been arranged by Charles Eugene Bedaux – who had lent them his house for their wedding – a French businessman who had major deals with German companies. Of dubious security background – he was suspected of spying for Germany in the First World War – Bedaux was trying to ingratiate himself with Hitler, who could open German markets to him, by arranging a meeting with a man Hitler had always wanted to meet. The Duke of Windsor's publicly announced reason for going to Germany was to study 'housing and working conditions', a subject that had always interested him as Prince of Wales and king, emphasised by his visit to South Wales in 1936. Edward's total disregard for British governmental and public opinion against the visit is likely to have come about because he was prevented from having a morganatic marriage, and because of the way his family treated his new wife and denied her royal status.

Several books have been written on the Duke of Windsor's supposed 'treachery' against king and country through his Nazi sympathies and the 'constant contact' the duchess had 'during Britain's dark hours' with Hitler's Foreign Minister Joachim von Ribbentrop (with the suggestion that the duchess had an affair with him). Moreover, Edward's reluctance to leave Paris in 1940 was interpreted in some quarters as Edward having knowledge of a German invasion of France and wherein he could have a base to negotiate peace between Hitler and Britain. While Edward was in Paris he presented a security risk; however, he then went to fascist Spain where his blatant passing of information to Hitler's diplomats in Madrid after the war had begun adding to negative public opinion. It was widely believed that Hitler thought that when (not if) he conquered the United Kingdom he could put a compliant Duke of Windsor back on the throne as a puppet king.

The German blood of the British Royal Family had been greatly researched by the National Socialists. To get the Windsors out of the way, and to stop them doing any diplomatic harm, on 9 July 1940 the wartime government of Prime Minister Winston Churchill appointed a reluctant Duke of Windsor as Governor of the Bahamas.

Despite the books denouncing the Duke of Windsor as 'a dangerous enemy of Great Britain', Francis Edward, 8th Baron Thurlow, Governor and C-in-C of the Bahamas 1968–72, speaking in 1999, summed up what many people thought about the Duke of Windsor and Germany:

> [Windsor] was basically taken for a ride. I don't accept at all that there was anything more than poor judgement [concerning his visit to Germany]: he was suckered into this situation, and he had nobody to advise him – no official staff at all.
>
> And [Windsor] enjoyed being made a fuss of: it's very difficult, if you've been made a fuss of all your life and then suddenly find that nobody is interested in you, so it's rather nice to be made a fuss of [as Windsor was by Hitler and his followers].

In the event of Hitler being successful in his conquering of the United Kingdom it is a matter of speculation whether or not the Duke of Windsor would have agreed to cooperate in the governance of his occupied birthplace, let alone agree to be its puppet king. Some four decades after his death the jury is still out.

The appearance of Prince Henry of Wales ('Harry') dressed as a Nazi soldier at a fancy-dress party in 2004 raked up memories and suspicions in the press concerning the House of Windsor's links to Hitler and their German background.

One of the most interesting of these links was HRH Prince Leopold Charles Edward, 2nd Duke of Albany, Earl of Clarence and Baron Arklow, born at Claremont House, Surrey, on 19 July 1884.

His parents were Prince Leopold, fourth son of Queen Victoria and Princess Helen of Waldeck-Pyrmont. Considered to be 'Queen Victoria's favourite grandson', he was educated at Eton. Yet his devoted grandmother dealt him a card that would seal his fate for ever. She decreed that he should succeed to the duchy of Saxe-Coburg and Gotha, from which German principality his grandfather Prince Albert had come.

So, aged 16, Charles Edward (now Karl Eduard) became duke of thousands of hectares of land in Bavaria and thirteen castles. Charles Edward was enrolled in the German Army (at the insistence of his overlord and cousin Kaiser Wilhelm II); the Kaiser then married him off to his own niece Victoria. When war was declared in 1914 Charles Edward had the nightmare situation of fighting for the Kaiser against the country of his birth.

By the end of the war in 1918 Charles Edward was declared a 'traitor' by his family in Britain and was stripped of his British titles. In his fear that Germany, now a republic after the deposition of the Kaiser, would fall to the communists, Charles Edward allied himself with Hitler and his National Socialists. Over the years he tried to develop good relations with Britain in the Anglo-German Fellowship, hoping that his cousin Edward VIII would develop his pro-German inclinations. All this came to an end on Edward VIII's abdication, and when George VI came to the throne relationships with Britain became icy for Charles Edward.

Under Adolf Hitler, Charles Edward accepted certain official positions. He was president of the German Red Cross, thus he presided over the programme of enforced euthanasia of around 100,000 disabled men, women and children all deemed by the Nazis to be a drain on resources. Still today the extent of Charles Edward's involvement is not clear. He turned up at George V's funeral in 1936 in military uniform, steel helmet and swastika armband. Again, war broke out in 1939 and once more Charles Edward opposed the land of his birth. His three sons fought for Germany and one, Prince Hubertus, was killed on the Eastern Front. At the end of the war Charles Edward was captured by the Americans and interned. Brought to trial for war crimes, he pleaded 'Not Guilty', and while dubiety was expressed he was 'exonerated of complicity in actual war crimes', but his estates were confiscated and he was fined heavily, forcing him into poverty.

Charles Edward died at Coburg on 6 March 1954. Ironically, his sister Princess Alice, Countess of Athlone, became one of the best loved of British royal ladies. She was deeply distressed at her brother's death but outlived him by some thirty years; she died in 1981 aged 98.

Other members of the Windsor's German family tree went along with Hitler, others held back. Queen Victoria's great-grandson Wilhelm of Prussia (b.1882), son of Queen Victoria's grandson Kaiser Wilhelm II of Germany, served in the 1st Infantry Regiment at Koningsberg; he played a role in the invasion of Poland but died from internal injuries in 1940 during an attack on the French positions at Valenciennes. His funeral at Potsdam drew a crowd in excess of 50,000 which displeased Hitler. The Crown Prince's brother, Prince August Wilhelm (1887–1949), became a keen member of the *Nationalsozialistische Deutsche Arbeiterpartei* (National Socialist German Workers party). At first Hitler was happy to accept the help and exploit the positions of German royalty, but by 1943 he turned against them and stripped all members of the Hohenzollern and Habsburg families of their titles and commissions. August Wilhelm was expelled from the Nazi party and arrested. Another who was thrown out was Queen Victoria's great-grandson Prince Wilhelm-Karl von Preussen (1922–2007), but a further four of Queen Victoria's great-grandsons were more committed Nazi supporters: the princes Van Hessen.

Prince Christoph (1901–43), his twin brother Richard (1901–69), Philipp (1896–1980) and his twin Wolfgang (1896–1989) had as their grandmother Princess Victoria (1840–1901), eldest daughter of Queen Victoria; she married Emperor Frederick II (1831–88) of Germany, King of Prussia. The princes' mother was Princess Margaret ('Mossy', 1872–1954), the youngest child of the Empress Frederick, who married Prince Frederick Charles of Hesse in January 1893. Prince Christoph married Princess Sophia (1914–2000) of Greece and Denmark on 15 December 1930. Her train was carried by her 9-year-old brother Philip (later Duke of Edinburgh). Christoph joined the Nazi party in 1931 and the *Schutzstaffel* (SS) in 1932; he was attached to Reichsführer SS Heinrich Himmler's personal staff and became head of Reichsmarschall Herman Göring's security service the *Forshungstamt*. Prince Richard joined the Nazi party in 1932 and the *Sturmbateilung* (SA) the same year. Prince Philipp joined the Nazi party in 1930 and the SA in 1932. Prince Wolfgang, also a party member, became Oberpresedent (governor) of Hessen-Nassau.

Queen Elizabeth II's marriage to Lt Philip Mountbatten (formerly Schleswig-Holstein-Sonderburg-Glucksberg), son of the bisexual Prince Andrew of Greece and Princess Alice of Hesse-Darmstadt, was almost scuppered by Philip's links with Hitler's henchmen. Leading the opposition to Philip, whose suit with the infatuated Princess Elizabeth was being doggedly pursued by Philip's uncle Lord Mountbatten, was his future mother-in-law Queen Elizabeth (better known today as the Queen Mother). One of her brothers had been killed during the First World War and she had a dislike of Germans, despite the fact that her own mother-in-law Queen Mary was wholly German. Nevertheless, she was opposed to her daughter marrying a man whose four sisters had married Germans and whose brothers-in-law fought for Hitler. Princess Elizabeth's deep infatuation for Philip Mountbatten meant that her parents, with serious misgivings, consented to the marriage. Philip's sisters and their husbands were not invited to the marriage ceremony.

At the diamond wedding anniversary celebrations of Queen Elizabeth II and Prince Philip, in November 2007, in the congregation at the Westminster Abbey service were a small group of Prince Philip's German relations; they were the prince's nieces and nephews, the children of his sisters.

Another link with the Nazi's came when Prince Michael of Kent married Marie-Christine, daughter of Baron Gunther von Reibnitz. The baron had honorary membership of Himmler's SS, but in the postwar de-Nazification most honorary-SS members were dubbed only *Mitlaufer* (fellow-travellers) and any public fuss concerning the marriage soon died down.

It was during the Nazi threat to Britain that Queen Elizabeth, the Queen Mother, became a sharp shooter. Apart from medieval monarchs who were brought up to bear arms, few modern British sovereigns have been marksmen off the hunting field. George V, Edward VIII and George VI all had naval training and were familiar with firearms. During the Second World War George VI learned how to use a hand gun and a sten gun. It is said that wherever he went during the war years the sten gun went too. From the early days of the war the Queen Mother was taught how to use a pistol, causing her to remark, 'Now I shall not go down like all the others'.

Did the House of Windsor leave their Russian royal cousins to be murdered?

'Ever your devoted cousin and friend.'
'God bless you good old Nicky.'
'You can always depend on me your greatest friend.'

Sentiments in letters from George V to his cousin
Tsar Nicholas II of Russia.

Secrecy in the Royal Family has been honed to a fine art. Yet often this concealing of the truth has led to misunderstandings and false rumours. One such 'cover-up' cited by historians is the supposed betrayal by George V of his cousins the Romanovs.

Shot at the Ipatiev House – the 'House of Special Purpose' – at Ekaterinburg, Siberia, on 17 July 1918, their bodies dumped in a mineshaft but later moved and buried; so died Tsar Nicholas II, his wife Tsarina Alexandra Feodorovna, granddaughter of Queen Victoria, and their five children. Their murders by communists have been well documented; and their exhumation in 1991 and reburial on 17 July 1998 in St Catherine's Chapel of St Peter and St Paul, St Petersburg, received international media coverage. But the role of the British Royal Family in offering help to their Russian cousins remains hazy.

In the weeks that followed Nicholas II's abdication of the Russian throne, for himself and his heir the Tsarevich Alexei, the future of the Imperial Russian Royal Family became a political and diplomatic conundrum. On 19 March 1917 the British ambassador in Petrograd (modern St Petersburg) was instructed to inform the Russian Foreign Minister, Paul Miliukov, that 'any violence done to the Emperor and his family would have a most deplorable effect and would deeply shock public opinion in [the United Kingdom]'. Miliukov enquired if the British government would grant the

Imperial Russian Royal Family asylum in Britain. The matter was discussed by Prime Minister David Lloyd-George, Chancellor of the Exchequer Andrew Bonar Law, George V's private secretary Lord Stamfordham and Foreign Office Minister Lord Hardinge. On 22 March signals were sent to the British ambassador to inform the Russian provisional government that the British would grant the Romanovs sanctuary for the duration of the war. These last few words were to be a clue as to the ultimate fate of the Romanovs.

Tsar Nicholas and his family took the offer at its face value; official discussions were made for the Romanovs to go to England. The family started to pack, expecting the call to embark at Petrograd quickly. Things were delayed as the royal children caught the measles. Back in Britain George V was having second thoughts. He was willing to arrange for his imperial cousins to seek sanctuary in say Switzerland or Denmark, but was increasingly 'doubtful' about them coming to England. George feared that temporary sanctuary would lead to permanent asylum. Once news had got out about the possible sanctuary offer, George received 'many abusive letters' from socialists and communist sympathisers and feared his kingdom might be plunged into bloody revolution. Sir George Buchanan, the British ambassador at Petrograd also 'pointed out that the presence of the Imperial Family in England would assuredly be exploited to our detriment by extremists as well as by the German agents in Russia'.

An alternative sanctuary in France was proposed and agreed by the British government, but not acted upon. The tide of events had quickened in Russia. On 22 March 1917, the Romanovs were moved to Tsarskoe Selo, near Petrograd, then to Tobolsk, Siberia, and then even further away to Ekaterinburg in the Ural Moutains.

In 2006 a diary was discovered that shed new light on a plot by the British Secret Services (then under 'C' – Sir Mansfield Cumming) to rescue the Romanovs. The diary belonged to

Captain Stephen Alley (d.1969, aged 93), second in command at the British International Mission at Petrograd; in those days Alley was employed by MI1, later MI6. The diary shows that Alley positioned a team of six fluent Russian-speaking agents ready to go to Ekaterinburg to rescue the Romanovs, codenamed 'The Valuables'. The plan was formulated to spring the Romanovs and take them by train to Murmansk and then on by Royal Navy vessel. The logistics were worked out but were never activated. Why? Historians believe, based on papers in the Russian State Archives, that Alley's telegrams detailing the rescue operation were intercepted by the communists (i.e. Bolsheviks) resulting in the house at Ekaterinburg becoming an impregnable fortress. Such a mission then would be military suicide. The Romanovs were left to their fate.

The British government had offered too little too late, and George V has never been exonerated for his part in procrastinating about what to do with his cousins. When Lloyd-George was writing his war memoirs in 1934, pressure was put on him to delete 'the chapter on the future residence of the deposed Tsar'. Lloyd-George complied. Did George V finally veto his cousins' rescue? The Royal Family still keep the answer secret. As Kenneth Rose wrote in his 1983 biography of George V: '… it is significant that the Royal Archives at Windsor contain hardly any documents dealing with the imprisonment of the Imperial Family between April 1917 and May 1918 …' So is it any wonder that researchers believe that another 'royal cover-up' was enacted to save George V's honour?

When it comes to the murdered Romanovs there has been some cooperation between the Royal Family and the scientists in trying to identify the rediscovered remains. When these remains were unearthed Prince Philip supplied DNA to help identify the skeletons. The Tsarina's niece Princess Alice of Greece was Prince Philip's mother. Even so, two skeletons were missing: those of the Tsarevich Alexei and his sister Maria. In 2007 more supposed

Romanov remains were discovered near the original burial site. Prince Philip's DNA has been cited again to prove that all the murdered Romanovs have now been identified.

Two postscripts to this story are of interest. One event is cited by some to underline what they consider to be King George V's 'hypocrisy' in the matter of his cousins' murder. Writing in her memoirs *My Dear Marquis*, Agnes, Baroness de Stoeckl, the former Miss Agnes Barron, wife of Sasha, a member of the Imperial Russian Diplomatic Corps wrote how Grand Duchess George of Russia (sister-in-law of Nicholas II) wished to hold a service in memory of her relatives at the Russian chapel in London's Welbeck Street. She wrote:

> King George and Queen Mary wished to attend.
>
> The little chapel was full when we arrived, all rose and bowed as the Grand Duchess George of Russia entered with her daughters and took her place on the right side of the Iconastasis [a screen shutting off the sanctuary on which icons were placed]. Seats placed next to her were reserved for their Majesties. We stood immediately behind her. She had asked for this.
>
> We were all in the deepest mourning, wearing the regulation Russian headdress, a Marie Stuart cap, the peak edged with white, a long crepe veil covering us from head to foot.
>
> Their Majesties entered, escorted by Sasha.
>
> The priests in their black and silver vestments appeared, they bowed low to the King and Queen then to the Grand Duchess …
>
> The beauty of the liturgy was too much for the loyal Russians who had come to pay their last homage to their beloved Emperor and all that he represented. They broke into sobs … Their Majesties were much moved and at the end, when the choir sang a prayer to the Virgin in farewell to the soul which had fled, tears were running down the Queen's face.

There were those in the congregation who thought the tears were 'crocodile tears'.

The British ambassador at St Petersburg, Sir George Buchanan, was criticised at the time for 'bungling' the safe passage of the Russian Imperial Family to Britain. Others thought that he was 'far too gullible' and had been 'hoodwinked' by the leaders of the Russian Revolution into believing that the Imperial Family would be safe.

Buchanan was humiliated and returned to England in 1918. He was warned by the Foreign Office to make no comment on the fate of the Russian Imperial Family or George V's role in it. If he did he would be charged with infringing the Official Secrets Act and would lose his pension. Although he went on to be ambassador to Rome from 1919–21, Buchanan was denied an expected peerage. He died in 1924 much embittered by his treatment over the fate of the Imperial Family; his relatives believed that he too had been muzzled to protect George V.

Why was George V's son called 'The Lost Prince'?

HRH Prince John, who has since infancy suffered from epileptic fits, which have lately become more frequent and severe, passed away in his sleep following an attack this afternoon at Sandringham.

Court circular bulletin from surgeon apothecary Sir Alan Reeve Manby
(1848–1925), 18 January 1919, Sandringham House.

Enter the lychgate of St Mary Magdalene church, Sandringham, Norfolk, walk forward and you will find him. His grave lies next to that of his baby uncle, another Prince John, the stillborn son of Edward VII and Queen Alexandra, of 16 June 1890. Who was this Prince John so interred in a grave that is remarkably un-royal and who biographers have called 'The Little Prince the Nation Forgot?'

Prince John Charles Francis was born at 3.05 a.m. at York Cottage, Sandringham, on 12 July 1905, the sixth and last child of Prince George and Princess Mary of Teck, the future George V and Queen Mary. All of the royal couple's children exhibited characteristic oddities. Prince Edward (the future Edward VIII) suffered from deafness inherited from his grandmother Queen Alexandra and was also a severe depressive, with the 'Hanoverian melancholic gene' inherited from his grandmother Queen Victoria. Prince Albert (later King George VI) had a distressing stutter and congenitally malformed knees. He would fly into uncontrollable rages. Prince Henry, Duke of Gloucester, had unfathomable fits of tears, interlarded with episodes of nervous giggling and was declared 'mentally backward'. Prince George, Duke of Kent, howled whenever he saw his mother, was of a 'frenetic character' and in adulthood was absorbed into a milieu of homosexuality and drugs. Princess Mary, later the Princess Royal, suffered from a crippling shyness, but had to be removed from her brothers' schoolroom for being a 'disruptive influence'. Alas, Prince John showed early signs of learning difficulties. At the age of 4 he began to suffer from fits, which the royal doctors diagnosed as epilepsy originating after conception (genetic epilepsy). His fits could render him violent and unpredictable, and when the royal children were out on the hills above Balmoral, for instance, Loeila Ponsonby noted, Prince John had to be roped to his nanny as a precaution against self-harm.

In an age when 'mental afflictions' were obscured from public view, it was noted that the Royal Family, said Garry Jenkins, 'wanted nothing more than to bury the memory of Prince John as an embarrassing footnote in their history'. Prince Edward, Prince of Wales, considered his afflicted brother a 'regrettable nuisance' and scarcely mentions him in his ghosted autobiography *A King's Story* (1951). Reginald Baliol Brett, 2nd Viscount Esher, political and royal go-between, noted Prince John's increasing unpredictability in his diary entry for 21 August 1910. On one occasion at lunch with the king and queen at Balmoral, wrote Esher, Prince John continually ran round the dining table 'all the while they ate'. Regularly he would slip from his nanny's notice to appear unannounced at his parents' official gatherings and make a 'scene'. As his behaviour became more eccentric, the king and queen realised that he was not controllable as 'normal' children; they were particularly concerned that John would have a fit in public. So, said the court gossips, John was packed off to Sandringham estate in the care of royal nanny Mrs Lalla Bill.

It is a popular royal description that George V and Queen Mary were unfeeling parents. Certainly the Duke of Windsor (the former Edward VIII) wrote to the Earl of Dudley after Queen Mary's death: 'I'm afraid the fluids in her veins have always been as icy cold as they are now in death.' Again, while jumping to the queen's defence, her lady-in-waiting of over fifty years, Mabell, Countess of Airlie, openly agreed that the queen 'had no interest in her children as babies'. Both George and Mary had a keen sense of public duty and in protecting the monarchy and this caused them to be secretive about John. He was moved to Wood Farm in 1916, on the edge of the Sandringham estate, near Wolferton. There, as far as the public were concerned, he became the forgotten member of the Royal Family. Perhaps the last family album photograph of him to appear in the public milieu was the one taken by Prince Edward at Balmoral in 1912, wherein Prince John is pictured riding in a metal royal car and sporting a white sailor suit. Despite the royal gossip about Queen Mary's coldness towards her children there is evidence that Queen Mary spent a lot of time with John at Sandringham, and his grandmother Queen Alexandra showed him much compassion. Despite her crippling deafness and rheumatism, she would send her car to Wood Farm to bring the 'dear and precious little boy' to her at Sandringham for afternoon tea, music and games.

Early on the morning of 18 January 1919, Dr Sir Alan Manby was called to John's bedside. Through the preceding night his condition had worsened after an epileptic fit. That afternoon Dr Manby recorded that John had succumbed to 'a severe seizure'. In her Sandringham diary Queen Mary wrote this:

> At 5.30 Lalla Bill telephoned to me from Wood Farm, Wolferton, that our poor darling little Johnnie had passed away suddenly after one of his attacks. The news gave me a great shock, tho' for the poor little boy's restless soul, death came as a great release. I broke the news to George & we motored down to Wood Farm. Found poor Lalla very resigned but heartbroken. Little Johnnie looked very peaceful lying there.

The queen penned another memory to her friend Miss Emily Alcock on 2 February 1919:

> For him it is a great release as his malady was becoming worse as he grew older, & he has thus been spared much suffering. I cannot say how grateful we feel to God for having taken him in such a peaceful way, he just slept quietly into his heavenly home, no pain, no struggle, just peace for the poor little troubled spirit which had been a great anxiety to us for many years, ever since he was four years old ... The first break in the family circle is hard to bear but people have been so kind & sympathetic & this has helped us much.

It is true to say that in an age of non-technological media, when newspapers were more reverential towards the Royal Family than today, by 1919 half of Britain had forgotten Prince John existed, while the other half had never heard of him. It is likely that Prince John had had the best care as prescribed by the medical and social criteria of the day. It is the modern interpretation of these criteria that makes John's 'exile' to Sandringham seem a chapter of royal embarrassment.

A little anecdote on Prince John comes from the memoirs of Baroness de Stoeckl:

One day [Princess Victoria, the second daughter of Edward VII] was in the nursery playing with her nephews and niece, the children of King George V. Prince John, the youngest, was only a baby, he had been given a piece of biscuit which he had sucked thoroughly, then scraped on the floor, finally he gave it to the dog to lick. At this moment, King Edward came in and stood looking down at the child. The latter held up the biscuit and said, 'Grandpa eat!' Before Princess Victoria could intervene, the biscuit had been swallowed by the affectionate grandfather. The princess, having seen the adventures of that biscuit, promptly left the room and was sick.

Acknowledgements

Each quotation in the text is acknowledged in *situ* and sourced in the Bibliography. In the compilation of the book many supplementary sources, too many to acknowledge separately, have been studied. In particular special mention is made of the author's gratitude to a sight of the biographical work on royalty undertaken by Mike Ashley and Dr Julian Lock in their *British Monarchs* (Robinson, 1998), and David Williamson in *Brewer's British Royalty* (Cassell, 1996). Royal anecdotes abound and the late Elizabeth Longford's *The Oxford Book of Royal Anecdotes* (Oxford University Press, 1989), and Deborah and Gerald Strober's selection of the oral history of Queen Elizabeth II, *The Monarchy* (Hutchinson, 2002) have been a useful source of reflection.

Every effort has been made to trace literary heirs of copyright material, but death of authors, reversion of rights and long forgotten publishing sources make the task more difficult. To all, though, many thanks are due.

Bibliography

Texts to 1800

Andre, Friar Bernard, *Vita Henrici Septimi*.

Anglo-Saxon Chronicle.

Anon., *Boke of Kervynge*, Wynkyn de Worde, 1508.

Bacon, Francis, *History of the reign of King Henry VII*, 1622.

Boorde, Andrew, *Brevyary of Health*, 1547.

Camden, William, *Annales Rerum Anglicarum, et Hibernicarum, regnante Elizabetha, ad Annum Salutis 1589*, London, 1615.

Capgrave, Friar John (1393–1464), *Chronicle*.

Chronicle of Pierre de Longtoft.

Chronicle of Walter of Guisborough.

Gaimar, Geoffrey (fl.1140), *Lestorie des Engles*.

Goscelin (fl.1099), *Translatio Sancti Mildrethe Virginis*.

—— (fl.1080), *Life of Saint Edward*.

Harrington, Sir John, *Metamorphosis of Ajax*, 1596.

Hazlitt, William, *Travel Notes*.

Holinshed, Raphael, *Chronicles* (England to 1535).

James I/VI, *Christis Kirk on the Green*.

Le Baker, Geoffrey, *Chronicle*, *c.* 1341.

Leland, John, *Collectaria*, pre-1548.

More, Hannah, *Daniel*.

More, Sir Thomas, *History of Richard III*.

Oglander, Sir John (1585–1655), *Diary*.

Paris, Matthew, *Chronica Majora*, (to the year 1253).

Philippe de Commynes, *Memoirs*, *c*. 1498.

Robert of Lewis, Bishop of Bath, *Gesta Stephani*.

Rous, J., *Historia Regum Angliae*.

Scalacronica.

Skelton, John, *Speculum Principis*, *c*. 1499.

Vergil, Polydore, *Anglicae Historiae*.

W.A., *A Book of Cookynge Very necessary for all such as delight therein*, Edward Allde, 1588.

Wace, *Roman du Rou*.

Wavrin, Jean de, *Chronique d'Angleterre*.

William of Malmesbury, *Gesta Regum Anglorum*.

Wolcot, John (Peter Pindar), *Poems*, 1791.

Worcester analyst, *Chronicle of the age of the Church*.

Selected Reading

Anand, Sushila, *Indian Sahib: Queen Victoria's Dear Abdul*, Duckworth, 1996.

Ashley, Maurice, *The English Civil War: A Concise History*, Thames and Hudson, 1974.

Barber, Richard, *Edward, Prince of Wales and Aquitaine: A Biography of the Black Prince*, Woodbridge, The Boydell Press, 2002.

Barlow, Frank, *Thomas Becket*, Weidenfeld & Nicolson, 1986.

Barrow, G.W.S., *Robert Bruce*, Edinburgh University Press, 1976.

Beatty, Laura, *Lily Langtry: Manners, Masks and Morals*, Chatto & Windus, 1999.

Benson, A.C. and Esher, Viscount, *The Letters of Queen Victoria 1837–1861*, John Murray, 1908.

Benson, E.F., *Queen Victoria*, New York, Barnes & Noble, 1992.

Bird, Anthony, *The Damnable Duke of Cumberland*, Barrie & Rockliff, 1966.

Bloch, Marc, *The Royal Touch: Monarchy and Miracles in France and England*, New York, Dorset Press, 1989.

Bomann-Larsen, Tor, *Folket*, Oslo, Cappelan, 2004.

Bradford, Sarah, *George VI*, Weidenfeld & Nicolson, 1989.

Brewer, Clifford, *The Death of Kings*, Abson Books, 2000.

Brewer, Revd E. Cobham, *Dictionary of Phrase & Fable*, Odhams Press, n.d.

Bridgeman, Harriet and Drury, Elizabeth, *Society Scandals*, David & Charles, 1977.

Broad, Lewis, *Queens, Crowns and Coronations*, Hutchinson, 1952.

Brodhurst, J. Penderel, *King Edward VII*, Virtue & Co., 1911.

Brown, Craig and Cunliffe, Lesley, *The Book of Royal Lists*, Routledge & Kegal Paul, 1982.

Chambers, James, *The Norman Kings*, Weidenfeld & Nicolson, 1981.

Chancellor, John, *The Life & Times of Edward I*, Weidenfeld & Nicolson, 1981.

Charlot, Monica, *Victoria: The Young Queen*, Blackwell, 1991.

Cheetham, Anthony, *Life & Times of Richard III*, Weidenfeld & Nicolson, 1972.

Cornwallis-West, George, *Edwardian Hey-Days*, Putnam, 1930.

De la Noy, Michael, *Windsor Castle: Past & Present*, Headline, 1990.

Dobson, Aidan, *The Royal Tombs of Great Britain*, Duckworth, 2004.

Doherty, Paul, *Isabella and the Strange Death of Edward II*, Constable & Robertson, 2003.

Dyson, Hope and Tennyson, Charles, *Dear and Honoured Lady: The Correspondence of Queen Victoria and Alfred Tennyson*, Macmillan, 1969.

Earle, Peter, *The Life and Times of James II*, Weidenfeld & Nicolson, 1972.

Field, Ophelia, *The Favourite: Sarah Duchess of Marlborough*, Hodder & Stoughton, 2002.

Fitzgerald, Percy, *Dukes and Princesses …*, London, 1882.

Fleming, G.H., *Lady Colin Campbell: Victorian 'Sex Goddess'*, The Windrush Press, 1989.

Fraser, Antonia, *King Charles II*, Weidenfeld & Nicolson, 1979.

—— *The Warrior Queens: Boadicea's Chariot*, Weidenfeld & Nicolson, 1969.

—— *Mary, Queen of Scots*, Weidenfeld & Nicolson, 1969.

—— *King James*, Weidenfeld & Nicolson, 1974.

Fraser, Flora, *Princesses: The Six Daughters of George III*, John Murray, 2004.

Frazer, Sir J.G., *The Golden Bough*, 1890.

Gairdner, James, *History of the Life & Reign of Richard III*, 1898.

Gillingham, John, *The Life & Times of Richard I*, Weidenfeld & Nicolson, 1973.

Gordon, Sophie, *Noble Hounds and Dear Companions*, Royal Collection Publications, 2007.

Green, David, *Queen Anne*, Collins, 1970.

Green, Shirley, *The Curious History of Contraception*, Ebury Press, 1971.

Grinnell-Milne, Duncan, *The Killing of William Rufus*, David & Charles, 1968.

Gristwood, Sarah, *Arabella: England's Lost Queen*, Bantam Press, 2003.

Hallan, E. (ed.), *The Plantagenet Chronicles*, Phoebe Philips Editions, 1986.

Hanrahan, David C., *Colonel Blood: The Man Who Stole the Crown Jewels*, Sutton Publishing, 2003.

Hibbert, Christopher, *George IV: Regent and King*, Allen Lane, 1975.

—— *Edward VII*, Allen Lane, 1976.

—— *George III: A Personal History*, Viking, 1998.

Hingley, Richard and Unwin, Christina, *Boudica: Iron Age Warrior Queen*, Hambledon & London, 2005.

Humble, Richard, *The Saxon Kings*, Weidenfeld & Nicolson, 1980.

Hutchinson, Robert, *The Last Days of Henry VIII*, Weidenfeld & Nicolson, 2005.

Kinnaird, George (ed.), *My Dear Marquis: Baroness de Stoeckl*, John Murray, 1952.

Lamont-Brown, Raymond, *Edward VII's Last Loves*, Sutton Publishing, 1998.

—— *Royal Murder Mysteries*, Weidenfeld & Nicolson, 1990.

—— *John Brown: Queen Victoria's Highland Servant*, Sutton Publishing, 2000.

—— *Royal Poxes and Potions: The Lives of Court Physicians, Surgeons and Apothecaries*, Sutton Publishing, 2001.

Lawson, M.K., *Cnut: England's Viking King*, Tempus Publishing, 2004.

Lee, Sir Sydney, *Queen Victoria*, Smith Elder, 1902.

—— *Edward VII*, Macmillan, 1925.

Leslie, Anita, *The Marlborough House Set*, New York, Doubleday & Co., 1972.

—— *Edwardians in Love*, Hutchinson, 1972.

Lindsay, John, *The Lovely Quaker*, 1939.

Loades, David (gen. ed.), *Chronicles of the Tudor Kings*, Greenwich Editions, 2002.

Longford, Elizabeth, *Victoria RI*, Weidenfeld & Nicolson, 1964.

—— (ed.), *The Oxford Book of Royal Anecdotes*, Oxford University Press, 1989.

Lowe John, *Edward James: A Surrealist Life*, Collins, 1991.

Luke, Mary, *The Nine Days Queen: A Portrait of Lady Jane Grey*, New York, Morrow & Co. Inc, 1986.

McClintock, J. Dewar, *Royal Motoring*, G.T. Foulis & Co. Ltd, 1962.

Macdougal, Norman, *James IV*, Tuckwell Press, 1997.

Madge, Tom, *Royal Yachts of the World*, Thomas Reid Publications, 1997.

Marlow, Joseph, *George I*, Weidenfeld & Nicolson, 1973.

Mason, Emma, *William II: Rufus, The Red King*, Tempus Publishing, 2005.

Masters, Brian, *The Mistresses of Charles II*, Blond & Briggs, 1979.

Melville, Sir John, *Memoires*, 1827.

Menkes, Suzy, *The Royal Jewels*, Guild Publishing, 1985.

Miller, John, *The Life and Times of William & Mary*, Weidenfeld & Nicolson, 1974.

Montague, Lord, *The Motoring Montagues*.

Morillo, Stephen, *The Battle of Hastings*, Boydell & Brewer, 1996.

Munson, James, *Maria Fitzherbert: The Secret Wife of George IV*, Constable, 2001.

Nicholson, Harold, *King George V: The Life & Reign*, Constable, 1952.

Parissien, Steven, *George IV: The Grand Entertainment*, John Murray, 2001.

Pendered, Mary Lucy, *The Fair Quaker: Hannah Lightfoot and her Relations with George III*, 1910.

Petropoulos, Jonathan, *Royals and the Reich: The Princes Van Hessen in Nazi Germany*, Oxford University Press, 2006.

Plowden, Alison, *Caroline & Charlotte: The Regent's wife & daughter, 1795–1821*, Sidgwick & Jackson, 1989.

Ponsonby, Sir Frederick, *Recollections of Three Reigns*, Eyre & Spottiswoode, 1957.

Prebble, John, *The King's Jaunt: George IV in Scotland, 1822*, Collins, 1988.

Priestley, J.B., *The Prince of Pleasure and His Regency*, Heinemann, 1969.

Reid, Michaela, *Ask Sir James*, Hodder & Stoughton, 1987.

Ridley, Jasper, *Napoleon III and Eugenie*, Constable, 1979.

Roots, Ivan, *Speeches of Oliver Cromwell*, Everyman Classics, 1989.

Rose, Kenneth, *King George V*, Weidenfeld & Nicolson, 1983.

St Albyn, Giles, *Queen Victoria: A Portrait*, Sinclair-Stevenson, 1991.

Seward, Desmond, *Richard III: England's Black Legend*, Hamlyn, 1983.

Sheppard, Edgar, *George, Duke of Cumberland: A Memoir of his Private Life*, Longmans, Green & Co., 1901.

Somerset, Anne, *Elizabeth I*, Weidenfeld & Nicolson, 1991.

Starkey, David, *The Reign of Henry VIII: Personalities and Politics*, George Philip, 1985.

—— *Elizabeth*, Chatto & Windus, 2000.

—— *Six Wives: The Queens of Henry VIII*, Chatto & Windus, 2003.

Steuart, A. Francis, *The Exiled Bourbons in Scotland*, William Brown, 1908.

Stewart, Alan, *The Cradle King: A Life of James VI & I*, Chatto & Windus, 2003.

Stoney, Benita and Weltzein, Heinrich C. (eds), *My Mistress the Queen: The Letters of Frieda Arnold, Dresser to Queen Victoria*, Weidenfeld & Nicolson, 1994.

Strickland, Agnes, *Lives of the Queens of England*, 1840–48.

Strober, Deborah and Gerald, *The Monarchy: An Oral History of Elizabeth II*, Hutchinson, 2002.

Taylor, Anthony, *Down with the Crown: British Anti-monarchism and Debates about Royalty since 1790*, Reaktion Books, 1999.

Thornton, Michael, *Royal Feud: The Queen Mother and the Duchess of Windsor*, Michael Joseph, 1985.

Tisdall, E.E.P., *Queen Victoria's John Brown*, Stanley Paul, 1938.

Tout, F.T., *Edward I*, 1890.

Turner, E.S., *The Court of St James's*, Michael Joseph, 1953.

Van der Kiste, John and Jordaan, Bee, *Dearest Affie: Alfred Duke of Edinburgh, Queen Victoria's Second Son,* Sutton Publishing, 1984.

Walvin, James, *Victorian Values*, Andre Deutsch, 1987.

Warren, W.L., *King John*, Eyre Methuen, 1961.

Warwick, Christopher, *Abdication*, Sidgwick & Jackson, 1986.

Watson, Francis, *Dawson of Penn*, Chatto & Windus, 1951.

Wedgwood, C.V., *The Trial of Charles I*, Collins, 1964.

Weir, Alison, *Elizabeth The Queen*, Jonathan Cape, 1998.

Williams, Ethel Carleton, *Anne of Denmark*, Longman, 1970.

Willson, D.H., *King James VI & I*, Jonathan Cape, 1956.

Windsor, The Duke of, *A King's Story*, Cassell, 1951.

Woodruff, Douglas, *The Life & Times of Alfred the Great*, Weidenfeld & Nicolson, 1974.

If you enjoyed this book you may also be interested in …

978 0 7524 9970 3

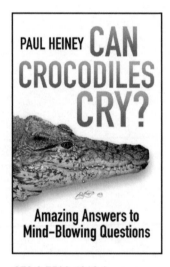

978 0 7509 6012 0